ROYAL THRONE

Royal Throne

THE FUTURE OF THE MONARCHY

ELIZABETH LONGFORD

ISIS
LARGE PRINT
Oxford, England

First published in Great Britain 1993
by Hodder & Stoughton, a division of
Hodder & Stoughton Ltd.

Published in Large Print 1993 by Isis Publishing Ltd,
55 St. Thomas' Street, Oxford OX1 1JG,
by arrangement with Hodder & Stoughton,
a division of Hodder & Stoughton Ltd.

British Library Cataloguing in Publication Data
Longford, Elizabeth
Royal Throne: Future of the Monarchy. —
New ed
I. Title
941.085

ISBN 1-85695-141-3

Printed and bound by Hartnolls Ltd, Bodmin, Cornwall
Cover designed by CGS Studios Ltd, Cheltenham

CONTENTS

Acknowledgements

Introduction

1 The Precedents 1

2 Crisis and Taxation 18

3 The Young Royals 43

4 How the Royal Family See Themselves . . . 68

5 How Others View the Royal Family 91

6 Updating the Monarchy 113

7 The "Magic of Survival" 150

Epilogue 180

Index 183

To Frank and our family,
all forty-four of them

ACKNOWLEDGEMENTS

By gracious permission of Her Majesty the Queen I have been allowed to quote from material in the Royal Archives. I would like to thank Mr Oliver Everett, the Royal Librarian, and Lady de Bellaigue for again being so very kind and helpful.

I am deeply grateful to members of the Royal Family and their staff for allowing me to consult them.

Many friends have been of great assistance but prefer to be unnamed; I thank them most warmly for their help.

My special gratitude is due to friends who have contributed to my understanding, some of them for the second or third time: Lord and Lady Charteris of Amisfield; Jacob Benthien, press counsellor of the Danish Embassy; Briony Binnie of the Education Department, Victoria & Albert Museum; Lady Butler; Roy Carne; Nigel Dempster; Lord and Lady Donaldson; Lord and Lady Dunsany; Lord St John of Fawsley; Alistair Forbes; Christina Foyle; Sir David and Lady Carina Frost; the Duchess of Grafton; Trevor Grove; Lord Hailsham; Antony Jay; Paul and Daniel Johnson; Douglas Keay; Andrew Knight; the Royal Borough of Kensington and Chelsea Libraries; the London Library; Lord McGregor of Durris; Suzy Menkes; Ferdinand Mount; Nigel Nicolson; Lady Powell; Paul Roche; Kenneth Rose; Mary, Duchess of Roxburghe; David Spanier; Mrs Jenny Tricker; Hugo Vickers; Barbara Winch; Robert M. Worcester of MORI; and Will Wyatt.

I owe a great debt to my publisher John Curtis, whose support has gone far beyond anything I had a right to expect; to Linda Osband, as always a superlative editor; to Michael Shaw my friend and agent; and to Douglas Matthews for another of his most skilful indexes. I must thank my family for positive help of every kind: Antonia and Judith for important suggestions after reading the manuscript; Harold Pinter for the story of Her Majesty's comment when opening an arts centre in East London named after him — "And quite right too!"; Thomas and Valerie for ideas and quotations; Rachel and Kevin for noble companionship on excursions, and introductions; Michael and Mimi for widening my European horizons; Kevin and Clare for encouragement when most needed; my granddaughters Rebecca and Flora, Maria and Eliza for continued cheerful interest; and Frank, not only for accepting my twentieth dedication, and reading and re-reading the manuscript, but also for bringing home armfuls of tabloids every day, having explained to anyone he met in the newsagent, "They're for my wife."

INTRODUCTION

We have entered what used to be called *fin de siècle* — end of a century. Because it is a chronological end, it seems to bring other things to a close as well. An older generation liked to speak of the 1890s as the Naughty Nineties, implying that the strict code of Victorian ethics was at last being seen off. Some of them denounced the change and called the age decadent; others welcomed the high kick on the stage, where long silken legs suddenly appeared from ruffled skirts like the stamens of exotic flowers. Today we are approaching the end not only of a century but also of a millennium. A Victorian hymn tells us that,

> A thousand ages in thy sight
> Are like an evening gone;
> Short as the watch that ends the night,
> Before the rising sun.

We are living in that last watch before daybreak. It usually begins as a peculiarly dark watch, the time of night — Dickens tells us — when the dying actually die. Conversely, the rising sun of the year 2000, some of us hope, is going to herald an age of brightness and change. Something a good deal better than a Channel tunnel with light at the end of it.

But now, still in the 1990s, we paint the last watch in peculiarly murky colours. We feel obliged to spot the maximum number of institutions that are dying and will never see the sun of the year 2000. In one week alone I counted four institutions and impulses that an ingenious press was putting on its "terminally ill" list: the ITN, Wimbledon tennis, sexual desire and the British Monarchy.

No matter that record crowds were to come out and celebrate a visit by the Queen to North Wales, or that 100,000 Canadians saluted her on Parliament Hill in Ottawa, the cry continued that the British Monarchy was crumbling. It had lasted 1,000 years and would never make it into its second millennium. As soon as Queen Elizabeth II ceased to reign, it was claimed, the whole institution would come to an end.

This prognostication, which sounds like an astrological rather than an historical prediction, would have appeared more convincing to our grandparents than it does to us. When the expectation of life was still only three-score years and ten, our Queen would have entered the last few years of her reign by the mid-1990s. How sad but how natural it would have been that the Monarch, the century and the second millennium AD should all go down together. Today, however, there is extended life expectancy, so it is possible that the Queen will live to be at least eighty or ninety years old. The reign of Elizabeth II is likely to continue well into the next century — other things being equal. This suggests, even on the pessimists' own argument, that the Monarchy will survive the gloomy events that the press's *fin de siècle* mood foresees.

My optimism does not spring from dyed-in-the-wool, lifelong monarchism, any more than the pessimistic feelings of some leading journalists spring from republican leanings.

Indeed, one senior journalist spoke to me about his "despair" of the Monarchy's survival, though he desperately longed for it to continue.

Brought up in a nonconformist family on both sides, I imagined that Church and State represented exclusion and opposition for the likes of us. One idea which never entered my head was that the country's contentious, divided people and interests could be held together by the Crown. I chose "Cromwell" as my subject for a school prize essay, and it was not until I was given Lytton Strachey's *Queen Victoria* as a history prize that I saw anything romantic, sad or funny about Victoria's reign. Before the publication of that seminal book, "Victorian" was a mere term of abuse, suggesting all that was inhibited, complacent and dull.

But for Strachey, politics would almost certainly have carried me into some kind of republicanism. When I first stood for Parliament as a Labour candidate in 1935, I remember including in my programme, "Abolition of the House of Lords". Though this, of course, did not necessarily mean abolition of the Monarchy, my feelings for the Royal Family were certainly confused by hearing on the wireless, just before a constituency party meeting, King Edward VIII's notorious announcement that life with "the woman I love" meant more to him than his crown and country. My first book was a rebellious attempt to expose the Jameson Raid in South Africa as a collusive plot emanating from British HQ, as represented by the Colonial Secretary, my great-uncle Joseph Chamberlain, a radical Liberal who converted to Tory Imperialism. I became deeply interested in Victorian politics and Victorian women. When an updated biography of Queen Victoria herself was suggested as the subject of my next book, the idea seemed inspired, provided I received permission to research in the Royal Archives, which I was fortunate enough to do. I still remember the shock of surprise and delight at the punchiness of Victoria's private letters. The dressing-down that she gave her grandson, the Kaiser, when he congratulated the South Africans on capturing the British raiders, seemed a model of how a royal matriarch should deal with an erring descendant.

During the four busy, exciting years I spent researching among Queen Victoria's family papers, I gained a consuming interest in Victorian families in general and the Royal Family in particular, developing a firm belief in the Monarchy's constitutional role. Apart from the fact that Victoria was a mother of nine (to my own eight), all of whom married and had children of their own (with one exception), she also embodied the Monarchy politically through a period of fantastic change. The first ever Education Act, for instance, was to introduce general literacy — a change in the potential relations of the people with their Government and Queen as great as that caused by mass television in this century.

It was fascinating to follow the thoughts of a shrewd but non-academic monarch, as Victoria strove unconsciously to break out from the mid-century restraints imposed on the Monarchy by the self-appointed royal adviser and editor of The *Economist*, Walter Bagehot. Magisterially, Bagehot had permitted her only three sovereign roles: to advise, to encourage and to warn. Nor did he think that any well-disposed monarch would want to go beyond these three. Nevertheless, Queen Victoria rightly felt in her bones that the country expected far more of her than Bagehot had laid down. After all, a good personal assistant or secretary performs all those three roles with great competence but without giving herself or himself regal airs.

George V, Victoria's grandson, was also solemnly tutored in the niceties of Bagehot. Yet he too, like his grandmother, knew full well that unless he could contribute something much subtler and deeper than advice, encouragement and warnings, he would never even begin to look like a great monarch. It is not Bagehot's fault that he has gone down in history as a somewhat superficial interpreter of royalty, when in fact he had many much more pointed things to say about it, as Lord St John of Fawsley's edition of his works amply demonstrates. Indeed, Bagehot was almost too keenly aware of the Monarchy's "mystic" role. However, among the generations that succeeded him it has been the fashion to minimise the magic, as analysed by Bagehot, and to emphasise *ad nauseam* the practical, secretarial roles. Yet, as we shall see, the Monarch has a role that is neither secretarial nor magical. Today Ferdinand Mount, editor of the *Times Literary Supplement* instead of The *Economist*, has tackled the received limitations of Bagehot most effectively, arguing that the Monarch's real role is to be guardian of the constitution.

Meanwhile, Queen Victoria and her family became increasingly complex and interesting the further I continued with my researches. She was an integral part of British history, with her own prejudices and preferences for other kings and queens. Denouncing George III and Queen Charlotte as bad parents, she romanticised the Stuarts, even though the only fatal break in her thousand-year dynasty was due to the mistakes of Charles I (over magic and money, otherwise Divine Right and Ship Money). It was intriguing to find that Victoria, who had given her name to the archetypal age of "family values" was instinctively a better queen than she was a mother. She did all the wrong things to her children (though not to her grandchildren), dishing out insults and showing favouritism, sometimes being guilty of neglect, at other times of possessiveness; yet such was the magnetism of her sovereignty along with her own personality that none of them felt they could live without her. And as Queen-Empress she set an example of racial and religious tolerance as well as sympathy with the poor at home that was admirable. (If they rioted it was always due, in her opinion, to "agitators".) Gradually I came to see the potential of Bagehot's illuminating phrase: "a family on the throne". Presidents, however remarkable as individuals, lacked that elegant and sustaining pattern of continuity; surely an incomparable boon to a head of state.

Individual kings and queens might lack personal distinction, but they were carried on the shoulders of the royal line. Given a suitable educational system, royal princes and princesses stood a better than average chance of performing their role in life successfully.

Making royal marriages was and is part of that role, for a hereditary monarchy must provide for the succession. I noted the figures for success and failure in the marriages of Victoria's nine children. Five of them were not only contented but happy (Vicky, Alice, Helena, Arthur and Leopold), all five marriages being virtually "arranged" and all contracted within the royal houses of Europe. Queen Victoria once remarked that marriage was always a "lottery"; but subject to that limitation, the ten young "royals" involved knew the rules of the game and played it accordingly.

Two of her children's marriages were unhappy, the one that was totally unsuccessful being Prince Alfred's. He made a spontaneous love-match with the Tsar's daughter, the grandest of all nine royal marriages. By contrast, the other unhappy marriage in the family was the least grand, but was not spontaneous either: that of Princess Louise to a commoner. Another contrast between this union and the other five was provided by the Prince of Wales's marriage to Princess Alexandra of Denmark. This was arranged and was not unhappy — at least for *him*. But only because Alix was exceptionally sweet-natured and, like her in-laws, played the game according to the rules, both to his and her own benefit. Finally, the marriage of Princess Beatrice to Henry (Liko) of Battenberg was definitely not arranged, but neither was its apparent happiness fail-safe. Perhaps fortunately, Liko's early death from fever while on the Ashanti expedition prevented possible infidelities from developing.

What does all this tell us about the future of royal marriage? One clear proposition seems to emerge from these Victorian statistics: marriages arranged by and for those who know the rules, and contracted by those who keep them, are likely to succeed. But, what are the rules?

Over the centuries the rules have changed radically. Anne Boleyn kept to the rules even on the block. Yet today it seems more shocking that she should have blessed Henry VIII at the moment of her execution than that she was executed. Her self-abasement was a horrible offshoot of the Divine Right of Kings, and it was to take until the reign of Queen Anne for that "divine right" to be dropped.

A second deduction can be made from the marriages of Queen Victoria's children: that royal love-matches were no less a lottery than others. Does this imply that a royal marriage, whether spontaneous or arranged, is in its very nature difficult? Dr Johnson pointed out that all marriages are difficult. How much more so a union destined to develop in a blaze or even a twinkle of limelight?

Incidentally, Queen Victoria assumed that the *scandal* of a broken marriage within her family could be created only by the unhappy parties themselves. She faced the fact that Princess Louise (her "darling Loosy") could not be forced against her will to live with her husband, the Duke of Argyll, for whom she had conceived a strong aversion, but she must not cause a scandal. In other words, the whole sad situation had to be kept quiet and the public kept in the dark. This was one of the rules of the game. For unless the parties themselves behave scandalously *in public*, no scandal need arise.

How Utopian and fanciful Queen Victoria's assumptions sound today, though for the 1870s and 1880s they made good sense. Britain's first Education Act was not twenty years old. Until all ordinary people could read, the press could not disseminate widespread scandal. However, the change was coming. By 1936 — some fifty years later — the Abdication was to require an amazing display of self-regulation by the press for it to go through as smoothly as it did. Appetites for scandal were hardly whetted before the whole thing was over. Another fifty years later and no such self-regulation is possible. The media, the press and the at-times prurient public have all combined to make the game and its rules as rare as royal tennis.

It will be the business of this book, among other things, to discover what, if anything, can be put in their place. However, it will not eliminate the possibility that Queen

Victoria's Rule 1 — exemplary royal behaviour — may still have its advantages.

I have said that my study of Queen Victoria's life and family gradually changed me from an incipient republican to a firm monarchist. At the same time, other experiences had combined with whatever historical imagination I possessed to increase my royalist convictions.

There was the funeral of King George VI in St George's Chapel, Windsor. A feeling of double loss swept in waves through that soaring Gothic greyness: the nation's loss of its king, the fiftieth monarch in an almost unbroken line of kings and queens, and the new Queen's loss of her father. The women of the Royal Family were all draped in long, black mourning veils, imparting an Arthurian strangeness to the wintry day, as if the mysterious queens of legend were about to carry the King away in a black barge. Such mourning veils would not be worn by any of us when a parent died, but they seemed in keeping with a head of state whose history went back into a past where history and legend met — beside affording some protection to the private grief of the King's wife and children. The perfection of the ceremony in its austerity and restraint finally wiped out the half-guilty impression I had formed of my own "Presentation" at Buckingham Palace twenty-two years before.

The whole ceremony was mainly for débutantes, but my section was known as "Presentation to Their Majesties upon Marriage". It must have been a trial to the then King George V and Queen Mary. And, to do them justice, they made no attempt to make it appear otherwise. I myself did not contribute any extra grace to the proceedings by curtsying so low that I almost failed to rise again from the royal carpet. Worse still, the preliminaries to this ceremony were nothing less than farcical.

The limousines occupied by us débutantes or young wives had to get into an infinitely slow-moving queue in The Mall and process for what seemed like hours round and round Queen Victoria's statue, until at last the great gates of the Palace were thrown open. My deb companion and I had been advised to bring a backgammon board to while away the nervous tedium. A photographer snapped the befeathered duo as we pretended to be absorbed in some winning or losing move. Next day I felt both amused and ashamed when my uncle by marriage, the Hon. Arthur Villiers, sent me a press-cutting of the scene, suitably inscribed by him with the words, "Socialites at play". He was a merchant banker with a social conscience, founding and living at the Eton Manor Club in London's East End, while I was to be a socialist candidate for Cheltenham at the 1935 general election. Socialist had become socialite. Bravely Queen Elizabeth II was to put a stop to the whole pathetic parade. It had had no more to do with the mystique or reality of monarchy than had the crowds who peered into our limousines and made faces at us — or we at them.

Totally different in effect and meaning was the Garter ceremony that I first attended in 1971 when the Queen honoured my husband by creating him a Knight of the order. This most ancient order of chivalry dates back to King Edward III. In the sole gift of Her Majesty, it is classless and meritorious. She can indeed count on the unqualified loyalty of her Knights, just as Edward III had done in medieval times. Nevertheless, the atmosphere of the Garter ceremony today is far from pompous. In the film *Elizabeth R*, celebrating the fortieth anniversary of the Queen's reign, we saw her waiting to process from the Waterloo Chamber to St George's Chapel. "Whoever invented these robes?" she smiled ruefully, as high winds took hold of the yards of blue velvet and whirled them around her while snatching at the ostrich feathers in her flat, black hat. I have always wondered how she keeps her balance on that long hill. Even Admirals of the Fleet have to tack, but she keeps her steady course.

In the same film we saw the Queen cracking a friendly joke at the expense of her ex-Prime Minister, Edward Heath. He was pointing out that while James Baker, the American Secretary of State, had not been allowed to visit the Gulf over Saddam Hussein's hostages, he himself had done so. "But then you're expendable!" exclaimed the Queen, teasingly. A few months later the expendable politician had become her new Knight of the Garter.

A few years before that date, at the 1989 Garter ceremony, I had had a chance to congratulate the Prince of Wales on his recent speeches on subjects of public interest, such as complementary medicine, architecture and the environment. I said I hoped that he would continue to express his deeply felt convictions in a forthright manner, which was what we wanted of a Prince of Wales. He looked pleased as he began to walk towards another group of his mother's guests. Suddenly he returned, to say with a wry smile: "Yes, but I don't want to be thought of as some sort of freak!" There are few blind spots in Prince Charles's vision.

A year later I was sitting next to the Duke of Edinburgh

at the Garter luncheon and, greatly daring, complained that his wildlife favourites could sometimes behave in an anti-social manner. Badgers, for instance, would come up from their homes in the woods every evening and lay waste a considerable area of my garden with their plumbing works. They preferred, apparently, that these things should go on in somebody else's home. The Duke took the point and laughed heartily, but without passing judgement on the badgers.

It is pleasantly ironical to think that a Whig prime minister, Lord Melbourne, cynically cited the Order of the Garter as the only honour that was in no way whatever earned. "I like the Garter", he said; "it has no damned merit about it." Nearly two centuries later people could point to the Garter as being one of the few honours left in which the merit is unquestioned. In any discussion of the Monarchy's future, the present honours system cannot escape notice.

Other events beside George VI's funeral and the Garter ceremonies have changed my understanding of a hereditary monarchy. As wife of a minister of the Crown, I was invited to the wedding in Westminster Abbey of Princess Elizabeth, and six years later to her Coronation. All eyes and thoughts were focused upon this woman who was dedicating herself, the first time to a man, the second to a nation. Each time I was impressed by the same thing: how serious, how absorbed, how carried out of herself she looked. I shall hope to show later that high seriousness is one of the Queen's greatest gifts. That is how a monarch should be.

A president may be full of lofty resolve at her initiation (I think of the splendid Mary Robinson, President of Ireland), but the dedication of a hereditary monarch must be more total. After all, presidents will have had other careers, whilst the heir to a throne is born for one thing only. Monarchy is a unique vocation.

Then there were my other insights (still under the guise of a minister's wife), whether at a royal ball, concert, banquet or garden party. After the initial sense of shock at being there at all — why me? — tempered by raging curiosity to see everything that was to be seen — the paintings, the porcelain, the clocks, the fellow-guests, the six-foot-tall delphiniums — I would settle down to enjoy the overriding sensation of pleasure: a feeling that we were welcome.

It was nothing personal. Everyone is treated the same. But all the members of the Royal Household, the cloakroom ladies and the staff in uniform seem pleased to see the visitor. It is as though they are saying, "You are at a party given by the Queen and her greeting recognises no difference in value between the highest and humblest citizen; she stands for all of you at your best. Welcome."

Of course we will all enjoy each scene in our own way. At the garden party, Peter Fleming, the author used to change into wellingtons down by the lake, and I once spotted him wading in to study some aspect of royal aquatic life. Gardeners would admire the magnificent herbaceous borders, all miraculously blazing with flowers at the same moment; others would discover the urns and statues that Cecil Beaton had used as a background for his photographs of Queen Elizabeth, now the Queen Mother. Some with tales of past intruders in mind would be fascinated by the outside walls and windows of the Palace; others again would note the small group of men and cameras on the parapet of the roof and wonder whether they were security or media. The rest of us would make for the marquees, hoping to meet up to a dozen friends, that being the average number for a royal garden party. The Queen, meanwhile, is genuinely concerned that her party will be a success, particularly that it will not rain, unlike her Uncle David (Edward VIII) who brought his boredom — and the garden party — to an end at the first raindrop. In unsettled weather I have sometimes observed a strange sight on the lawns outside the tea-tents: groves of gentlemen's rolled black umbrellas stuck into the green grass with a grey top hat balanced on top, looking like ancient Turkish tombstones. I hope the royal gardeners blame the countless holes in the lawn on London starlings.

Since my *Victoria R.I.* was first published in 1964, I have written six more books on the Royal Family. Any book involving research is certain to teach the author more than the author will teach the reader. That wonderful storehouse of royal and national biography, the Archives at Windsor Castle, has been a constant source of surprises, all of which affected my views as I progressed through the House of Windsor from Elizabeth II to Lady Antrim, the lady-in-waiting, to Queen Elizabeth the Queen Mother, to royal anecdotes, to the letters of Princess Louise. I do not have space to enumerate all the discoveries I made over the years. However, I can take this early opportunity to illustrate some of the curious patterns that emerged from my studies in royal biography. I shall stick here to the minor examples, leaving the ones that bear directly on the future of the Monarchy to the relevant chapters of the present book.

For instance, no royal rumour is too improbable for it to be widely and eagerly believed. When it reaches the public zone, it will endow pure lies with the aura of "a reliable eye-witness account". I was struck dumb for a moment by the report that

Princess Margaret Rose as a child was a deaf mute, until I remembered the historical fact that Queen Victoria, when a small princess living quietly in Kensington, was said to be a cripple who could not walk. One wishes that the "deaf and dumb" Princess Margaret could have had the chance to tell her detractors what she thought of them; they might have preferred to be deaf themselves.

The question of royal love affairs belongs to later chapters, but invented royal love children frolic through the pages of Victorian, Edwardian and modern history and journalism. It was no shock, therefore, to discover that the childless Princess Louise, Queen Victoria's fourth daughter, had allegedly given birth to two babies by separate fathers, neither of them her husband. After all, did not Queen Victoria herself have a fictitious son by her gillie, John Brown, who lived in Paris to the age of ninety? When I was known to be researching a life of the first Duke of Wellington, I would regularly receive letters from well-intentioned families who had grown up with "a strong tradition" that the Duke was their ancestor. Their evidence? Some was convincing, being based on documents; others pointed out that for generations the family had sported exceptionally large, hooked noses. These were not lies but honest legends. It is fortunate, however, that, so far, royal Hanoverian descent has not been claimed by every family with a genetic tendency to protruding eyes and a turned-down mouth.

Most royal rumours are pretty uncomplimentary, as indeed are the majority of rumours that attach themselves to public characters. But with royalty it is occasionally the other way round. They may be saddled with flattering stories that seem to enhance their virtuous characters but in reality detract from the more interesting truth. I had always been put off by the saintly account of Queen Alexandra's making her final self-sacrifice to King Edward's unfaithfulness. According to the story, as soon as she realised that the King was on his deathbed, she sent for his mistress, Mrs Alice Keppel, threw herself weeping into Alice's arms and then left the field to her successful rival. The truth was a good deal more human. It turned out that Alexandra was far too spirited — and incidentally too devoted — to abdicate voluntarily from her rightful position as wife at the eleventh hour. She did indeed summon Alice Keppel, as instructed in an old letter of the King's, allowed Alice to say goodbye to the unconscious King, and then firmly said goodbye to Alice. Outside Alice had hysterics. Alexandra's behaviour had been impeccable, but less sentimentally romantic than the legend would have us believe.

Another aspect of the Monarchy that changed beneath my eyes as I pursued my researches, was the idea of the Royal Court and Household. At first I found myself adopting the usual stereotyped picture of courtiers. They were obsequious, sycophantic, reactionary and only of average intelligence. Yet here was Queen Victoria's famous private secretary, Sir Henry Ponsonby, whose letters and sayings soon put a stop to such unreal analysis. Born into a noble Anglo-Irish family, with a touch of that carefree originality which had infused Lady Caroline Lamb (*née* Ponsonby), he courageously put the Liberal side of British politics to a Victoria becoming daily more Conservative. It was also a credit to her that she allowed him to do so.

Sir Michael Adeane (later Lord Adeane) held the post of Queen Elizabeth II's private secretary when I was writing

Victoria R.I. He added to his first-class degree at Cambridge a character that was never afraid of firm action. It was he and the Queen herself who insisted on her daring visit to Ghana in June 1961, which the Government had tried in a weak-kneed way to call off, alarmed by the possibility of terrorism. The tour went off without a hitch.

Sir Martin Charteris (now Lord Charteris) had become the Queen's private secretary before I began my *Elizabeth R*. An artist in sculpture and words, he was the first to suggest a shot of humour in the Queen's speeches, realising, as no one else did, how perfectly adapted was her own style of dry wit to the occasional joke.

Incidentally, one of the best jokes to emanate from King Edward VII's Coronation originated in the Royal Household. When a special stall was constructed in Westminster Abbey to hold the King's lady friends, it was christened by the Household the "Loose Box". Later I shall have more to say on the Royal Household in relation to the Monarchy's future.

I would like to touch upon one problem that has faced me during the writing of this book but was absent from all the other books I have written. I finished my biographies of the Queen and of the Queen Mother with the former's Silver Wedding and the latter's eightieth birthday. But though I would not have hesitated to predict that many fruitful years lay ahead of them both, I never for an instant expected a series of extraordinary events to occur in their lives the moment I had written the last pages. With *Royal Throne*, begun at the end of May 1992, the scenario has been quite different. Perhaps I should briefly describe how the book came about, or my problems might sound unreal. My publisher commissioned me to write a short book of general interest on the Monarchy's prospects, as an institution, in the next century. Having accepted this stimulating but not sensational proposal, I promptly sent letters to personages and friends I knew in the world dealt with by my future book, asking them for interviews. My letters anticipated no difficulties, but they must have arrived on my friends' desks on the very same day as the news broke of Andrew Morton's book on the Princess of Wales and its serialisation in the *Sunday Times*. They were all kind enough to believe me when I said that I had written to them without the slightest suspicion of what lay in store. I asked my publisher if he had had prior information or second sight. "There were rumblings", he replied. (I had not heard them.) But apart from this chronological ineptitude — or aptitude, whichever way you look at it — there was a second problem arising from the first.

How much of the gossip, speculation, invention, scurrility, fiction and odious fact was relevant to my book? I have never before had to construct a volume in which the raw material suddenly slid away from under my hand or alternatively came pouring in from unsuspected sources. As a result, I have had to leave some decisions to the last possible moment, returning to several chapters for partial rewriting. In retrospect, it is all too clear why the unfortunate Queen called the year 1992 her "*annus horribilis*". Living through a crescendo of disturbing experiences must indeed have made it a horrible year. It culminated in dramatic events that had to be charted here one after the other with scarcely a pause: the burning of Windsor Castle, the financial announcement and the separation of the Prince and Princess of Wales. It would be rash to predict a series of "wonderful years" after that horrible one; indeed, the beginning of 1993 with the "Camillagate" tape may be described as *"horribilissimus"*. But there are surely grounds for hope of better things, as well as for caution. In the words of Edmund Burke, the eighteenth-century thinker, "I have done no more than state the case. Many things occur."

Though the Queen reiterated her impression of a "sombre" year of "difficult days" in her Christmas message for 1992, nevertheless she made a point of ending on a heartening note. She had met and talked to the heroic and dedicated Leonard Cheshire at an Order of Merit dinner shortly before his death, and she saw him as the embodiment of what she herself passionately believed in:

> Kindness in another's trouble,
> Courage in your own.

CHAPTER
ONE

The Precedents

This is making history. This is what I like.

*Stanley Baldwin to his private secretary, Thomas Dugdale,
after the Prime Minister's last dinner with Edward VIII
before the Abdication, 1936*

People have suggested that anything written from now on about the future of the Monarchy requires a question-mark, but the sub-title of this book is a statement not a query. There are no convincing arguments to suggest that the British Monarchy is about to be wound up — wound up by Parliament, of course, for that would be the constitutional way of doing it. Or perhaps our small band of home-grown republicans — "Fun Republicans", as Dr John Casey called them in the *Sunday Telegraph* — expect a violent "Fall of the Palace" on a par with the storming of the Bastille, the British mob leading out King Charles III, blindfolded, to the foot of Queen Victoria's statue, where justice would be done in the name of the sovereign people. Or again, humane republicans like the writer Sue Townsend may simply envisage some relevant version of her own royal satire: removal of the royals to a Midlands' council estate, where most of them would merge painlessly into the disadvantaged lives of their former subjects.

The prospect of the electorate appointing a president or acquiring a dictator in place of their constitutional monarch seems extremely remote. It would indeed be strange if Britain voted out its Monarchy just when the monarchical idea in Europe was having a new lease of life. A look at Denmark later will make the point; not to speak of Spain, which restored the crown seventeen years ago, having experienced abdication, a republic overthrown in a terrible civil war, and dictatorship. It may turn out that the British and Spanish constitutional monarchies have something to learn from each other. Meanwhile, the ancient British model shows no signs of being dismantled, lock, stock and Balmoral. Reforms there may be, must be. But all the lessons of the past should point to an improved performance by the Crown rather than a muddled, ignominious exit from the national stage.

We as a nation take pride in the amazingly long history of our Monarchy. It has lasted for over a thousand years, even if we begin the line with Edgar as the first king of all England (959–75), rather than with either of the two earlier claimants to that distinction, Eadred (946–55), or Edward the Elder (899–924). However, the royal line is not particularly remarkable for the superior quality of its individual kings and queens. Its most impressive feature is its continuity. In other respects the total of fifty sovereigns are much like other people of their period: good in parts. The chief difference from other people is that the bad were worse than normal, because of their greater opportunities. There were a few great sovereigns like Edward III, Elizabeth I and Victoria. There was one royal saint, Edward the Confessor, and another possible saint, Henry VI. But what of the overall picture?

We have got to make room for the vicious and the victims, murderers and those they murdered, usurpers, adulterers, drunkards, gamblers, a carrier of haemophilia and perhaps a porphyriac, and maybe a syphilitic. Has their presence in the royal line fatally weakened it?

Fortunately for these black sheep, the idea of a *model* royal family did not develop until the reign of Queen Victoria. To be a model, and a model on a family scale, is beyond the capacity of most human groups. But even the idea of the single person, the reigning hereditary monarch, possessing outstanding qualities is difficult enough to achieve. Yet the individual sovereign has always been expected to be father and protector of his people, "lord and warrior"; an anointed and therefore a spiritual leader; of striking appearance; and with luck (or clever court painters) of "godlike" beauty. Come to that, is god*like* strong enough? (The word was first applied to King Athelstan, 924–39, and then to Edward III and Henry VIII.) By reason of their so-called "divine right" to rule, kings were held to share something of divinity itself. At least, according to Shakespeare, they had a permanent divine "hedge" around them. Who could tell exactly what the human creature was like who lived behind the hedge? Surely it was not flatly human? Judging by their reputed power to cure the King's Evil (scrofula) with a simple touch of the hand, kings could achieve wonders denied to mere mortals. True, the royal "touching" sessions were officially dropped after the reign of Queen Anne, but they still have their echoes even in this modern age. The American public had a passion for touching Edward VIII when he was Prince of Wales, while the present Princess of Wales is reported to believe in her own special gift of healing. (This, of course, may not be connected with her royal status, though it seems to date from her marriage.)

Granted that the Princess may never have made any such claim — and we know that tabloid inventiveness will go to all lengths — the fact that it has been stated in print shows that tabloid readers are expected to believe it. We are all free to agree or disagree that certain people exhibit paranormal powers of healing. That is not the argument here. The point is that for over a thousand years the British people have believed that their monarchs possessed a special something. That something has ranged from quasi-divinity to the admirable "example" set by three out of five monarchs this century: George V, George VI and Elizabeth II, as against Edward VII and Edward VIII. Yet if we examine the actual records from the past, the results are frequently found to be pointing in the opposite direction; in other words, to something deplorable. In fact, the Monarchy has survived despite its past history, which is too often mad, bad and dangerous to know.

If more than average human virtue, attended by average good luck, had been seriously required of each and every one of our sovereigns, the royal line would hardly have lasted into the modern period by more than a thousand days. As for the antics of certain younger members of the Royal Family in the late twentieth century, they would have seemed positively trivial compared with the Monarchy's lurid past. And yet that crime-laden, doom-ridden line has endured from the tenth to the twentieth century.

Our present trouble is that there has developed a kind

of contraflow. The expectation of royal virtue is far higher today than it ever was during its first nine centuries, whereas the actual record of divorce and stable marriage among the general public is much lower. The Royal Family is expected to behave better than most of their ancestors did at a time when the rest of us are behaving, at least in regard to sexual morals, worse.

There are four possible solutions to this modern dilemma of the Monarchy: to lower our expectations of the Royal Family, particularly in regard to stable marriage; for them to raise their actual standards all round; to get rid of those within the royal circle who break the rules; and to get rid of the whole institution of Monarchy — throw away the babies, the bath-water and the bath itself. My crystal, or rather perspex, ball tells me that the first three of those solutions will be tried to some extent, but the fourth? No. And why is that last desperate throw ruled out? The answer must be that the idea of a monarchy has always been more important than the facts of royal lives. Good behaviour gives it strength; bad behaviour of whatever sort has had only a passing effect. Let us look in detail at the past, remembering that facts are powerless compared with ideas and feelings.

Six kings have come to an "ignoble" end, as contemporary historians put it. They were murdered: Edmund, brother of Athelstan, murdered by his stepmother; Edward the Martyr, son of Edgar; Edmund Ironside; William Rufus; Edward II and Edward V, the elder of the two "Princes in the Tower". Add to them three ill-fated queens: Mary, Queen of Scots, mother of James I, and two of Henry VIII's wives, all three executed. Two other kings may have been murdered, John and Henry VI. The deaths of eight more kings were untimely:

5

Harold, Richard I and Richard III killed in wars; Richard II deposed; Edward VI struck down in youth by tuberculosis; Charles I executed; James II exiled; and William III thrown from his horse. Nor was the royal line free from other grave misfortunes at every stage. Anne had no surviving heirs, and illness, it may have been porphyria, destroyed the much maligned George III.

If personal behaviour is in question, we can point to four usurpers — Stephen, Henry IV, Edward IV and Henry VII; three kings with male "favourites" — Edward II, James I and William III; and too many mistresses and bastards in all periods to enumerate. Even the "good" kings had mistresses, Edward III's mistress stealing the royal rings on his death-bed. Eadwig quitted his Coronation banquet for the company of whores; all Harold's children were illegitimate; Henry I had a record number of bastards; and some of the mistresses of Charles II and Edward VII were as famous as their royal lovers — Nell Gwynn and Barbara Villiers, "Jersey Lily" and Alice Keppel. George III was the only Hanoverian monarch whose domestic life was considered impeccable. All the other male Hanoverians had their German or British mistresses, William IV producing a family of ten by the delightful actress Dorothy Jordan and then discarding her for a royal marriage of convenience with the German Princess Adelaide. Actually it was far from convenient, for the royal couple had no surviving heirs.

With this historical background it is not surprising that recent royal misbehaviour has seemed to many people a storm in a stirrup cup. However, others — like Michael Fathers in the *Independent* — have gazed into their crystal-style ball and foreseen "a packed but subdued House of Commons" listening to the Clerk of the House announcing in medieval French "that the Queen had given her consent to the Republic of Great Britain and Northern Ireland". *La Reine le veult.* (Fathers dates his vision to "an evening in the next century"; and as the Queen would have reached the age of 100 by 2026, he probably envisages the republic arriving within the next twenty years.)

However, I see the royal nightmares of the early 1990s producing quite a different outcome.

Divorce, separation, marriage-on-the-rocks have all bathed the Court in their baleful light. However, the year 1992 was different from any other year when marital troubles had afflicted the Royal Family. Princess Margaret's divorce in 1978 made people feel, if anything, guilty rather than shocked. Had not their own Government prevented her from marrying her first love, Peter Townsend, simply because he was a party — the innocent party — to a wartime marriage and divorce? Lord Harewood's divorce from his first wife and the birth of a son to his second wife before their marriage were said to have greatly upset the Queen, but few were aware of this at the time. Princess Anne's divorce had been preceded by such devoted service to the world's threatened children that public respect for the devotion had swallowed up their regret for the divorce. Nevertheless, this case did step up the royal divorce figures. In 1992 news, some of it shamefully obtained, of two more royal marriages breaking or broken was to have a totally different effect. Newspapers began totting up the numbers. Three out of the Queen's four children in trouble; and past cases of splits, which were beginning to be forgotten, now helped to swell the cheerless statistics.

Reckoning the Royal Family to consist of the widowed Queen Mother, the Queen and her Consort, the Prince and Princess of Wales, Princess Anne, the Duke and Duchess of York, Prince Edward, Princess Margaret, the Kents, the Gloucesters and Princess Alexandra, the public could see all too clearly that the royal figures for unhappy marriages were likely to be no better than the thirty per cent national average. What sort of model family was this? Learned people were consulted about the possible legal effects of unsuccessful marriages within that concentrated magic circle. What were the precedents for divorce?

At first sight it seems absurd to question the existence of divorce within the Royal Family. Every child, even the unlucky one who learns no history at school, has heard of Henry VIII and his six wives: two divorced, two beheaded, one died, one survived. Both Henry's divorces were technically annulments. His marriage to Catherine of Aragon was ended on the grounds that she had been his deceased brother's wife, when marrying your deceased brother's wife was forbidden by the church. Catherine retorted that her former union with Prince Arthur had never been consummated — she was still "a maid" when she married Henry. Less theological reasons for Henry's action were that he passionately desired a legitimate son and equally passionately desired Anne Boleyn. Each of these desires, he felt, would be satisfied after divorcing Catherine and marrying Anne. Henry's second divorce was from Anna of Cleves. This time it was Henry who claimed that the marriage had not been consummated, owing to Anna's plainness that — in modern slang appropriate to this Monarch — had never "turned him on".

Another point that needs making in regard to Henry VIII's annulments may somewhat alter modern attitudes to precedents for royal divorce:

> ... it must be appreciated that divorce was by no means such an unthinkable prospect, nor such an uncommon occurrence then in the 16th century as is sometimes supposed. Looking no further than Henry VIII's own family, we find that both his sisters were involved in somewhat murky marriage arrangements. . . .*

Queen Elizabeth II has herself drawn attention to the occurrence of royal divorce, this time in the twelfth century. On her visit to Bordeaux in 1992, she pointed out, in a speech delivered in perfect French, that Eleanor of Aquitaine was divorced by Louis VII of France and then married to Henry II of England. "She did not give her second husband an easy time either," added the Queen dryly, as if pointing out that marital discord was nothing new.†

Coming nearer home, to the year 1870, Bertie, Prince of Wales, the future Edward VII, found himself in the divorce court. Subpoenaed by counsel for the defence, the Prince narrowly escaped censure in the notorious Mordaunt case in which his friend, Sir Charles Mordaunt, accused his young wife of adultery, naming two members of the "fast set" as co-respondents. Both were also friends of the Prince. Fortunately, the dozen letters that the Prince himself had written to the lady proved to be trivial rather than erotic, and the lady herself had become insane. Bertie denied having

---

*Antonia Fraser, *The Six Wives of Henry VIII* (1992), p. 133.
†*Majesty*, August 1992.

committed adultery with her. Nevertheless, his reputation could not but be damaged with both his family and the public. Princess Alexandra was deeply pained, while Queen Victoria felt that he had been wildly "imprudent" and was mixing with the wrong people: members of high society who were leading "frivolous, selfish and pleasure-seeking lives".

After the Mordaunt case the Prince of Wales was involved in three other *causes célèbres*: the Aylesford scandal (1876), the Baccarat case and the Beresford case (both in 1891). All four scandals had one thing in common: the heir to the throne, though not personally guilty of relevant misconduct on these particular occasions, was the intimate associate of people who accused each other of adultery or cheating at cards.

The Aylesford scandal might have resulted in the Prince of Wales being subpoenaed for the second time, now in a divorce case brought against his wife by Lord Aylesford, which cited Lord Blandford as co-respondent. Lord Randolph Churchill, Blandford's brother and Winston Churchill's father, threatened to have read out in court some compromising letters he possessed from the Prince to Lady Aylesford, which, if published, "would ensure that His Royal Highness would never sit upon the Throne of England". Churchill's attempt at blackmail was a bluff — the Prince's letters were relatively innocent, though he had had a flirtation with Lady Aylesford — but it was true that another appearance in court would have done the Prince no good.

Again subpoenaed as a witness in the Baccarat case, the Prince was to hear counsel implying that his client (Sir William Gordon-Cumming, the alleged cheat) had sacrificed himself "to support a tottering throne or prop a falling dynasty. Such things had been known." Queen Victoria privately deplored her son's example, which was "so bad".

At the centre of the Beresford marriage scandal was the fascinating socialite, "Daisy" Brooke, later Lady Warwick and the hostess at Easton Hall to left-wing socialists.* Once more it was a compromising letter that set the drama in motion. Daisy had written it to Lord Charles Beresford and Lady Charles had given it to a solicitor. Could the Prince of Wales get it back for Daisy? He could not, but he did succeed in getting Daisy as his lover.

At the time of the Mordaunt case, Mr Gladstone, Queen Victoria's great Liberal prime minister, had found himself forced to consider whether the throne was still secure. All was well, he decided, as long as the country still had confidence in the Queen's personal character — which it did. But it was "only half a century ago", wrote Gladstone, that another royal divorce scandal had rocked the throne. If memories of that event were revived by scandals like the Mordaunt case, the throne must be weakened and might be overthrown.

What past event was Gladstone thinking of? By dating it to about 1820, he showed that he was comparing the possible effects of the Mordaunt divorce case with King George IV's attempts to divorce his wife, Queen Caroline. The King had been humiliated in every possible way: the House of Lords' "Bill of Pains and Penalties", which was intended to lead to Caroline's divorce by the King, failed to win sufficient support and had to be dropped; Caroline

*I was once a weekend guest.

11

had become the favourite of the London crowds; soldiers mutinied; and George himself was so much insulted and reviled that he hardly dared put his head out of doors. If the wretched Caroline had not died a few weeks after George IV was crowned without her, his Coronation might conceivably have been followed by forced abdication.

Abdication in fact, with no ifs or buts, is still at the time of writing the most traumatic royal event of the twentieth century. Hitherto, unsuitable heirs to the throne have been removed as if in obedience to some providential decree. Edward VII's eldest son, Prince Eddy, was a weak character suspected of connections with the notorious Cleveland Row scandals, involving male prostitutes. Fortunately, Eddy died young of pneumonia. The second son then stepped into his shoes, becoming Prince of Wales, marrying Eddy's fiancée and occupying, as George V, what would have been his brother's throne. Again, it was a second son, George VI, who rescued and stabilised the throne in 1936. So striking was the "second son" syndrome that the historian, Paul Johnson, has been tempted to work out a general theory that goes like this:

In history the heir apparent was spoilt from the first moment of his life. Therefore there was very little chance of eldest sons making good monarchs. But second sons, or those who fought for the throne, had a better chance. Edward III had to do battle for the crown and made a good king. Henry V spent some time in exile in France — and made a good king. Henry VIII was a second son and good king. Charles I was a second son and had a good character. George V — second son, good king.

But the prototype of all spoilt, over-indulged, flattered eldest sons and heirs was — Edward VIII.*

The fairy tale of David and Wallis — the Prince Charming who was gobbled up by an American siren who turned him into a frog — is too well known to need repeating. However, certain details of the story are highly relevant to any study of the Monarchy's future. On the face of it Mrs Wallis Simpson was less to blame than King Edward VIII. Her only public misdemeanour had been to go twice through the divorce courts. Repeated divorces, though still fairly rare in Britain, were commoner in America and could not be taken as a sure sign of depravity. The King's being head of a church that appeared not to cater for divorce did, indeed, present a problem, but those who supported his intention to marry Mrs Simpson had their solutions. Edward could resort to the old-fashioned Continental practice of the morganatic marriage, or he could get crowned first in church and married afterwards, the public having meanwhile become acclimatised to Wallis. Edward refused to contemplate coronation without her at his side as his anointed queen.

Divorce was not the deepest, though it was the most cutting, argument against her. "Unsuitability" — a word that would be heard frequently in the 1990s — could be applied to Wallis on a wide front. Being American was not necessarily part of it. She was unsuitable principally because she had not the faintest idea of what the Monarchy meant.

*Paul Johnson believes that the late Lord Mountbatten, Prince Charles's beloved great-uncle, was concerned lest the talented Prince should be spoilt. Johnson also thinks that the present Royal Family needs an elder statesman, such as Mountbatten was, to advise them.

After she had become Duchess of Windsor she passionately wanted to add the words "Her Royal Highness" to an already exalted title for the sake, she said, of the extra "chic". It was as if the British Monarchy were a superlative fashion house of which she would, in a sense, be queen, while her rival, Queen Elizabeth, could still be referred to as "Cookie" in embittered letters to Edward. By penning these vulgarities, Wallis proved herself unfit to be a royal highness let alone a queen, while King George VI's wife was about to be wafted aloft in her crinolines, towards a fairy-tale future.

On the other hand, Edward knew a good deal, though not everything, about the duties of kingship. In this knowledge he deliberately chose romantic love rather than duty. Millions of his countrymen had in the past sacrificed life as well as love for their country in war. Millions were soon to do so again. He, too, was brave, ready to die for his country, but not brave enough to live for it "without the woman I love".

The part played by the Royal Family in the long-drawn-out crisis is also of interest. They all stuck together, led by the Queen Mother who was then Queen Mary. This gave the reluctant new Monarch unexpected personal strength. They all dreaded having to curtsy to Wallis, perhaps giving a more important place than would be given today to deference. Jokes against "Mrs S" were more to their taste: for instance, that she would only ever sit on one "throne".

The part played — or rather, not played — by the press in 1936 is a point for comparison with our own period. If King George VI had had to cope with the modern tabloids as well as with his brother's furious telephone calls about finance and other sensitive subjects, he might not have pulled through. Throughout the manoeuvres and negotiations, one tabloid would surely have launched a powerful "Anti-King Party", showing a photograph of a lightly clad Wallis idling in the arms of her regal lover, while another tabloid, to restore its circulation, would have caught "Bertie" (George VI) looking drawn and distraught as he confessed to his cousin Dickie Mountbatten, "I am only a naval officer. I don't want to be King."

As it was, a gentlemen's agreement between Lord Beaverbrook and Lord Rothermere (Britain's two powerful press lords, the former a Canadian) managed to keep the Abdication out of the public prints until the worst was over. With no such agreement, respect for the Monarchy would have been punctured by indiscretions and lies. Yet it is said that today's gentlemen of the press, instead of being proud of their profession's self-regulation in 1936, are thoroughly ashamed, regarding it as a humiliating failure in their investigative and informative duty. One thing is certain: a "gentlemen's agreement" will never happen again, at least not on the scale of Abdication year, 1936.

Finally, how far should we accept the Abdication as any kind of precedent?

There is no doubt that King George VI, his family and friends were all flying danger signals. A storm like an abdication had to be taken very seriously and could foul the very anchors of monarchy. Take the disputed question of the Duke and Duchess of Windsor's wedding in 1937. Walter Monckton, the Duke's private secretary, wanted at least the Dukes of Kent and Gloucester to attend it; but Clive Wigram, the King's private secretary, said that if they did it would be "a firm nail in the coffin of the Monarchy". Then there was the argument against the Duchess's HRH. If in the future, wrote Wigram, the Duke of Windsor had to divorce the Duchess (as Wigram fully expected) and she bore her title away with her "as a choice fragment of her alimony", how would the Monarchy look? King George VI felt that, "The Monarchy has been degraded quite enough already." No doubt he would have used the same words if he could have foreseen the Yorks' divorce half a century later.

On the general question of how the Monarchy as an institution emerged from its battering by the Abdication, opinions hardly differ. It was stronger than ever. At the same time there is room for dispute as to why this was so.

To begin with, the distinction between the Monarchy as an institution and the individuals who make it up has always been well understood, particularly by the Royal Household. The point is vividly illustrated by a collection of letters from this period. In 1927 the wife of Alan ("Tommy") Lascelles discussed with her husband the case for his resigning as private secretary to the Prince of Wales (later Edward VIII). "I have no illusions about, and not much respect for, your Chief," she wrote, "but if you think it is all worth working for as an institution, and part of the country — then I think it's worthwhile." But if he thinks it is of no great importance how the Monarchy is run, he must resign on the grounds either of another "urgent job", or, quite straightforwardly, on the grounds of the Prince being "a hopeless rotter". Lascelles resigned, but was reappointed by King George VI after the Abdication.*

Some believe that the people simply glided smoothly into

---

*In Royal Service: The Letters and Journal of Sir Alan Lascelles, ed. Duff Hart-Davies, vol II, pp. 20–36.

their new role as subjects of George VI instead of Edward VIII, without a tremor. Others give the credit to the new family, a model family of four; particularly to the parents' heroic efforts to create a sense of national family during the Second World War.

"How do you think I liked taking on a rocking throne," wrote George VI to his brother, the ex-King, "and trying to make it steady again? It has not been a pleasant job, and it is not finished yet."*

Through the resilience of the institution and the strength of his personal efforts, he finished the job and bequeathed his success as a precedent for dealing with future troubles.

It is time to turn from precedents to the present.

*3 July 1937, quoted in Philip Ziegler's *King Edward VIII* (1990), p. 361.

CHAPTER TWO

Crisis and Taxation

In short, that argument about the Monarch's tax exemption is small beer. There are many ways in which the cost of the Monarchy could be reduced, if Parliament felt that Britain no longer needed a Rolls-Royce royal family.

The Economist, 25 January 1992

When I decided to write about the House of Windsor in 1977 there was little interest in the future of the Monarchy, except from a small band of enthusiasts and personal friends. "Yes," the majority of people seemed to say, "write about the Monarchy by all means, but don't expect to have any influence on the country's future. It's a slice of history, agreed, and anyway you can't burn your fingers on it."

Only sixteen years later all the bland complacency has changed. The Monarchy has become a talking-point, often a passionate subject of argument. Perhaps "crisis" is still too violent a word to apply to an ancient institution like the Monarchy that has surmounted so many worse threats. Even so, words like "crossroads" and "transition" are definitely in order.

The area of crisis, if such it was, had gradually built up in the middle of 1992 from a variety of different danger zones: the uncomfortable memory of recent royal divorces, an astoundingly short-lived royal marriage already heading for the same solution ("They didn't try"), the revelations of the Princess of Wales's friends, the unbecoming conduct of the younger generation, whose personal lives seemed neither royal nor responsible, and the taped telephone conversation known as "Dianagate". However, it is doubtful whether any or all of these unhappy events would in themselves have been enough to push or drag the Monarchy into deep crisis. The turning-point came when criticism of a divorcing monarchy led on to denigration of a costly crown. Throughout June and July 1992 the tabloids and broadsheets hungered only for news of the Princess of Wales and the Duchess of York. But by September the question of royal taxes had begun to occupy the whole press. Paradoxically, it looked as if the tax question, despite its having arisen mainly in the wake of marital troubles, would be the only one to have a lasting effect on the Monarchy of the future.

The way the tax question came to the fore is evident from a few contrasted press-cuttings on finance. Anthony Holden, the author, reviewing a royal TV documentary in The *Independent* on 7 June, began quite boldly but, after testing the temperature of the water with one toe, quickly withdrew his foot. After calling the programme "revealing and well-documented", he explained that the production company had set out to prove nothing less than "the Queen's misuse of public funds for private gain". But already his courage failed him. "*If it didn't quite manage it* [my italics]", he proceeded, "it raised important and damaging questions along the way."

Three days later (10 June) A. N. Wilson, writing in the

Evening Standard, told the Queen shortly and sharply how to put her house in order: "She should announce forthwith that she alone, with her consort, will draw money from the Civil List." She should then offer "as a gesture of goodwill", to pay income tax, while the public in turn should ask the media to give them less news of the Royal Family. This latter point is a controversial issue. For if the House of Windsor took a sabbatical and "bowed out" for a year, say, the public might not invite them to bow in again.

Seven weeks passed and on 30 August the columnist Janet Daley was more forthright than either of her male colleagues. "The recent poll that showed a startling 80% disapproving of the Queen's tax-free status", she wrote, "suggests that there is more than prurience at work in the public's appetite for royal exposure." Daley thought the deeper causes were the recession, producing resentment at royal wealth, and discontent with the system of privileges.

However, by the end of September some of the press seemed to have felt that the criticism was going too far. Up till that date it had been quite common to refer dogmatically and sometimes quite angrily to the Queen as "the richest woman in the world". But then the *Daily Mail* pointed out that Her Majesty came no higher than number ten in a list of Britain's female Croesuses. "Old Money Rules", announced the *Mail*'s headline, meaning by "old money" inherited wealth; "but the Queen's £100 million takes only 10th spot."

Should the Queen pay taxes? This question was one of the most likely to be used as a selling-point in the press after the brouhaha of late summer and autumn 1992. Yet it already embodied an elementary misunderstanding. The

Queen did pay some taxes like the rest of us. She has always paid value added tax and all indirect taxes. She has also paid customs duty on her purchases abroad. What she did not pay until 1993 was tax on her private income and capital. The confusion between income tax and the rest is typical of the tangle existing in the minds of the press and public. As the Prince of Wales has remarked with patient exasperation: "Misunderstanding of the situation is *enormous*. People understand the basics but have no idea of the details."

The Duke of Edinburgh once said that voluntary change was the life-blood of the Monarchy. Does that include changes in taxation? The purpose of this chapter is to clear away the misunderstandings, so that it may be possible to consider what changes would be acceptable.

It may be argued that in a study of the Monarchy's whole future the side issue of its financial status should be made to wait for a later chapter. On the contrary, royal taxation has gradually become of central interest. Since the 1970s, the whole tone of discussion has changed. First and foremost, taxation is one of the few subjects today on which the Queen has been criticised — and criticised by a more nearly unanimous public opinion than is shown on any other aspect of the modern Monarchy.

"Forty years on the throne and not a foot wrong" — that had been the regular tribute to Queen Elizabeth II as she celebrated her fortieth anniversary. True, in her youth a pin was stuck between her dazzling wings by John Grigg, who, having got his butterfly on to the board and under his microscope, perceived her personality to be that of "a priggish schoolgirl . . . a prefect, recently a

21

candidate for Confirmation".* Harold Nicolson, author of her grandfather George V's official biography, judged that Grigg's criticism had given Elizabeth II strength. Today the comparison of the Queen with a school prefect is no longer pejorative. Hugo Vickers, an articulate monarchist, credits her with:

> . . . a youthful enthusiasm combined with a sense of authority, a good judgment of right and wrong, this wish to inform, this wish linked with a certain expectation that her listener will note and remember what she has said. Is it best summed up as the attitude of head girl at a British public school?

Again, there has been political criticism of the Queen's allegedly biased handling of the "hung" Parliament in 1974, but this was convincingly rejected on television in September 1992. Her general performance will be examined when the Monarch's role as Head of State is reached. Meanwhile, alongside this rare instance of her impartiality being challenged go numerous examples of her ingrained neutrality, as between the political parties. Her own private life is impeccable, her popularity impressive, her world-wide recognition and appreciation unique. Why then, in the very year of her fortieth anniversary as Queen, did this sleeping dog awake? From his kennel marked TAXPAYER the animal came out growling. He barked outside neighbouring kennels marked HM AUDITORS. Soon there were confused sounds of dispute. What had stirred the taxpayer into angry activity after over twenty years of relative quiescence?

*It is not easy at first to see the point of the analogy with a "recent candidate for Confirmation". Then one remembers that just four years earlier the young Queen had been anointed at her Coronation.

It was after the serialisation of Andrew Morton's book in the *Sunday Times* that the monetary mountain erupted. Suddenly the Princess of Wales, as portrayed in Morton's *Diana: Her True Story*, had dragged down the Royal Family to the level of each and all of us. And she herself, from having been an "example" to follow, a goddess to worship, a Princess Nightingale to admire, had become a victim to be pitied, thanks to a pitiless Royal Family. Princess Diana and her children were presented as the victims of a cold husband and uncaring father whose friend and confidante of twenty years, Camilla Shand, later Parker Bowles, was said to have got between him and his young wife and family. The Princess's own old friend and confidant, James Gilbey, had told Morton that Diana was unable to put out of her mind the "one-time relationship" of the Prince and Camilla. Gilbey added: "As a result their marriage is a charade. The prospect of Camilla drives her spare." Camilla had first met the Prince twenty years before and, with characteristic wit and love of a joke, had recalled to him that she was the great-great-granddaughter of Alice Keppel, King Edward VII's mistress — "How about it?" Next year, 1973, this good-looking, spirited "county" girl married the Prince's close friend, the popular cavalry officer Andrew Parker Bowles, now a brigadier in charge of Veterinary and Remount Services and formerly the Queen's Silver Stick in waiting. Camilla's many interests include country sports, watercolour painting and architecture. Prince Charles is godfather to the Parker Bowles's eighteen-year-old son.

Three of Princess Diana's female in-laws who also come under Morton's lash are the Queen, the Queen Mother and Princess Margaret, described as "an implacable troika";

while Diana's father-in-law, Prince Philip, was allegedly so small-minded as to be jealous of his own heir.

Why then, went the argument, should we, the taxpayers, pour out the monstrous millions that the Royal Family would receive every year for a decade which had started in 1990? The taxpayers were in a mood to feel hard done by, if suitably encouraged. Not only were they enduring economic recession — the worst since the 1930s, when at least it was honestly called a slump — but yet another of this "right royal" clan had already abandoned her husband and was asking for a divorce. And so the press cashed in on the new pseudo-crusade: the mission to punish the Queen and all her brood by changing them at long last from tax-avoiders to royal taxpayers.*

Admittedly the resentful tone of the above reflects the feelings of those who were republicans in any case or were indifferent to the Monarchy. Both groups were temporarily joined by a larger section of the public who believed that a taxpaying Queen would in fact strengthen the Crown. It would make a bond of union between Her Majesty and the people, forging a new link in the democratic chain. Among the many young people of thirty and under whom I questioned as to whether the Queen should pay income tax or not, every single one said "Yes".

The next move must be to discover how the royal tax position came about.

One key is 1910, the first year of George V's reign. David Lloyd George, the Liberal Chancellor of the Exchequer

---

*R. H. S. Crossman, "The Royal Tax-Avoiders", *New Statesman*, 1970.

and terror of the aristocracy, rose in Parliament to make a notable statement on the King's Civil List (expenses), which at that date, along with his income, was taxed. It was illogical, argued the Chancellor, to tax the Civil List. It would be "giving with one hand and taking away with the other". What was the point of reimbursing the Sovereign for expenses incurred in the performance of his public duties if part of it was to be clawed back again by the Treasury? Since 1910, taxation of the Civil List has rightly been dropped.

Inconsistently but fortunately for the Crown, taxation of the royal Duchy of Lancaster was also dropped at some point after 1910. Why was this inconsistent? Because the Duchy's revenues were (and are) paid into the Privy Purse as part of the royal income, not as expenses, and therefore in theory at least were taxable. And why was this inconsistency lucky for the Crown? Because it re-established the royal prerogative and established the Crown's *de facto* immunity from income tax.

The next key dates are 1936–52. Some time in the early 1930s negotiations had been opened between the King's advisers and the Inland Revenue on the whole principle of whether the Sovereign should pay income tax. The result was that exemption for King George VI was agreed on some date between the beginning and end of the King's reign. The minutes of these discussions, leading up as they did to the exemption of Queen Elizabeth II and her successor (unless the law was again changed), are unfortunately not available for scrutiny. In answer to a question from a Labour MP in 1991 a Treasury minister replied: "This file appears to have been destroyed in 1977."

It is probable, however, that the negotiators went back to an even earlier key date than 1910 in the history of royal finance — namely, 1842. This was the disagreeable moment for the young Queen Victoria (aged twenty-two) when Sir Robert Peel, her second prime minister and first Tory prime minister, asked her to contribute to the new tax — income tax. Peel paid his unwelcome visit to the Palace on 16 March, explaining how the radical Lord Brougham had demanded in Parliament that not even "the highest in the land" should be exempt. The Prime Minister therefore pressed the Queen to pay three per cent, adding as an extra inducement that her uncle King George IV had decided to pay ten per cent when income tax was levied during the Napoleonic wars. What could Victoria do but agree? Nevertheless, there was always her private journal in which she could give a more accurate picture of her feelings. On the same evening she wrote in its pages that the new income tax was "rather hard" on her and "very hard" on "my poor dear Albert", who would have to pay £900.

Five days later Victoria was considering a posthumous request from Lord Munster for the continuation of pension payments by her, the Queen, to his family. Munster was the eldest (illegitimate) son of King William IV and, therefore, Victoria's first cousin, one of the "fringe royals" who were a constant drain on her privy purse. She had been paying him £1,200 a year (£24,000 in today's money). Now he had shot himself and, in his will, wished the pension to be paid to his children. Peel was shocked. Lord Melbourne, her beloved ex-prime minister and a Whig, advised her not to pay, otherwise all semi-royal persons would be applying for money, as well as genuine royalties. (Sure enough, on

6 November the Queen was having a long talk about the £17,000 she paid to "the Aunts", Princess Sophia and the Duchess of Gloucester.)

On the same day, 21 March 1842, Melbourne, prompted no doubt by Munster's application, wrote a long letter to Her Majesty warning her against too much generosity towards the State. Her agreement to pay income tax was right, he thought, in that it would be very popular, "which in the present circumstances of the country [it had entered the so-called Hungry Forties] and state of public feelings is a great advantage". But did Her Majesty realise that she was giving up a constitutional prerogative, which "has hitherto exempted the Sovereign from all direct taxation"? Besides being "a great pecuniary sacrifice", it would make "a great change in her circumstances, which can only be repaired by care and economy".

Readers may recall that the press of 1992 more than once used Queen Victoria as a stick to beat her great-great-granddaughter with. Pointing a finger of scorn at Queen Elizabeth II, they would quote the alleged "fact" that "Queen Victoria *volunteered* to pay income tax", the implication being that even a less than democratic sovereign of a century and a half ago had done better by the public than our own modern Monarchy.

If Victoria was a "volunteer", God help the unwilling taxpayer. Let us hope that this story will not go down to posterity as one of those pseudo-revelations that a glimpse into history itself can so quickly unmask.* Meanwhile, we

*Peel gave the first impression of Queen Victoria's "volunteering" by telling Parliament: "it was her determination that her own income should be subjected to a similar burden" as her subjects.

must turn to the first change in the royal tax arrangements during the reign of Elizabeth II.

Over twenty years ago, on 22 November 1971, Her Majesty's Stationery Office published a Blue Book on the Monarchy's finances. Beginning with the Report by a Select Committee on the Civil List, it then went on to print the evidence taken by that Committee between 21 June and 27 July. In the present study of the royal finances, the order of the narrative will be reversed: first the evidence, then the decisions announced in the Report. Incidentally, this was the first time that evidence had been published.

One preliminary point may also be noted. The tone of the 1971 Report is remarkably different from the sometimes malicious, strident and unpleasant atmosphere of today's discussions.* Not that the members of the 1971 Committee agreed with each other's political opinions. There were left-wing MPs like Harold Wilson, Douglas Houghton, Roy Jenkins and an out-and-out republican, William Hamilton, the Scottish scourge of the Crown. On the right were such stalwarts as Norman St John-Stevas and John Boyd-Carpenter. There was no hint of sourness or envy, although, now and then, the members of the Committee would tease each other. In fact, the royal finances were not a gnawing subject of contention, dividing the nation. No Duchess of York had appeared to expect a no longer docile but highly cynical public to continue to pay for her frolics.†

*Edward VII had found the Select Committee of his day "difficult to manage". Elizabeth II's was far from unmanageable.

†In reverse, the *Sun* newspaper was boasting on 10 October 1992 that it

My quotations from the evidence are necessarily selective, since the Report covers 166 pages, including appendices.

There is a fundamental difference between this Select Committee on the Civil List and any other that is likely to be convened today or in the near future. Then, the Queen was asking Parliament for the Civil List to be increased; now Parliament would be requesting the Queen to increase her payment of taxes.

The first thought in many minds was, if the Queen's private fortune was so vast, was an increase in the Civil List really necessary? As if to pre-empt such thoughts, a "Gracious Message" from Her Majesty was read out in Parliament by the Chairman on 21 June 1971:

> Her Majesty has been much concerned by the astronomical figures which have been bandied about in some quarters, suggesting that the value of these funds [HM's private resources] may now run into fifty to a hundred million pounds or more. She feels that these ideas can only arise from confusion about the status of the Royal Collections, which are in no sense at her private disposal. She wishes me to assure the Committee that these suggestions are wildly exaggerated.

The passage of time has done little to impede the reckless course of rumour and wild exaggerations are still being bandied about. Even Philip Hall, author of an exceptionally well-researched book called *Royal Fortune* (1992), gives

had made the Duchess of York pay her four months overdue builder's bill of £3,746.76: "SUN MAKES FERGIE PAY UP."

exaggerated accounts of the Queen's wealth: there is mention (on page 159) of her being "far and away the richest person in the country" with 3.25 thousand million pounds (quoting *Money* magazine) and making reference (on page 234) to the Queen's "vast fortune".

A more extraordinary thing is that almost exactly the same confusion still reigns today. In press discussions about the Queen's wealth, such items as the Crown Jewels, the Royal Collections of paintings, plate, porcelain, furniture and the Royal Archives (bequeathed to the Crown by William IV), should, strictly speaking, not be mentioned at all in this connection, since they are inalienable (the Queen has no right to sell them). The fire at Windsor Castle in November 1992 was an example. It was pointed out that the buildings belonged to the nation. Many people assumed, however, that because the Castle was the Queen's official residence, its contents belonged to her personally and their restoration should be paid for by her. Unfortunately, articles on Her Majesty's wealth nearly always begin by naming the Crown Jewels, and if, later on, they are relegated to a separate category of possessions, the damage has already been done and confusion created in the public mind. At most the Collections should be included in a footnote or bracket, or, better still, firmly excluded by name from the beginning.

After the "Gracious Message" of 1971, evidence was called on various aspects of the royal expenses, such as the gardens and the staff. For example, the Committee was told of a scheme to train ten young students a year in the royal gardens.

The Royal Household and staff were weightier matters,

because the Queen's increased public expenditure was largely due to inflation resulting in a general rise in staff wages and salaries, and to increasing royal activity between 1953 (Coronation year) and 1970. William Hamilton suggested that, "perhaps some of the staff are willing to serve at low wages because of the status symbol considerations. Is that so?" Lord Cobbold (Lord Chamberlain) replied: "It would be nice if they would, but I have not seen any indication of it, quite frankly." Cobbold added that it was his job to see that "from top to bottom people are properly paid". Hamilton (probably expecting, even hoping for the answer "No") continued: "Are there shop stewards in the Palace?" Lord Tryon (Keeper of the Privy Purse, otherwise, Treasurer)* answered: "Yes." In fact, a new pay claim by the Civil Service Union, on behalf of the Palace staff, was already in the pipeline.

Joel Barnett (Labour) asked a question about the 208 entirely unpaid staff: "Do you think it right that you should have that amount of unpaid staff?" Cobbold responded: "I think so, yes. . . . They are happy to do it and they regard it as a service to The Queen, the Crown, and, indeed, to the State, I think." It turned out that these volunteers operated only occasionally, for instance at garden parties, investitures and state visits.

At last, through the questioning of Jeremy Thorpe (Liberal), Lord Cobbold reached the area he really wanted to discuss. Thorpe had asked him about his projection as to increased costs in the years ahead: "Is it a year-to-year

---

*Philip Hall is not averse to an occasional joke. Of the Queen's Keepers of the Privy Purse, he writes, one was called Tryon and the next Blewitt (Sir Ralph)!

budget or is there a five- or ten-year projection of what likely costs are going to be?" Cobbold replied: "We at the Palace are very much hoping that some method will be found which will automatically, or semi-automatically, cover the increased portions of expenditure."

It was to be this natural wish on the part of the Queen and the Palace not to go to Parliament every year for an increase in the Civil List that eventually — though not until 1990 — induced the Prime Minister, Mrs Thatcher, to fix the Civil List for ten years ahead. It could then be adjusted if and when necessary.

Meanwhile, Sir Robin Turton (Conservative) wanted to know how many foreign nationals worked on the Palace's domestic staff? Russell Wood (Deputy Treasurer to the Queen) said: "I am guessing, but I think probably twenty at the outside. . . . They come and go with lightning rapidity." Douglas Houghton thought that there were so many foreigners because British workers wanted more pay, but it turned out that there were only twelve altogether, four of them from the Commonwealth; the other eight were mostly Spaniards, working in the kitchens. Later on Joel Barnett was told by the General Secretary of the Civil Service Union that most of the housemaids were British and pretty well organised, but there was "weakness" in the kitchens.

A more sensitive subject soon came up with the auditing of the Civil List. This was the duty of Parliament, through the Treasury. Though it was generally agreed to be difficult to distinguish between the Queen's public and private expenses (she paid personally for the Palace uniforms, for instance), the Household was extremely cautious about putting anything on to the Civil List. When Lord Tryon was asked whether it was "a deliberate policy to err, err, shall we say, on the side of caution as to what is put up for Civil List consideration," he replied, "Oh, absolutely, I would say quite definitely."

Despite this extreme caution and the many reforms in the operation of the Civil List, including the removal of "archaic" practices in 1964, the Civil List was in the red. And it had been in the red since 1962. Although the amount voted by Parliament was supposed to be adequate enough to remain unchanged from the beginning to the end of any one reign, the vote had already proved inadequate only ten years after a probably long reign had begun. As Charlie Pannell, a trades union MP on the Committee, put it, "I understand that what we are looking for, or what the Palace is looking for, is something in the nature of £450,000 a year at the end of next year [1972]." Russell Wood agreed: "That is the deficit."

At the mention of the actual figure, the atmosphere in the Committee changed, though its members all knew that figure full well. Suggestions for a new royal deal poured out. Harold Wilson and Jeremy Thorpe both proposed similar radical changes in the administration of the Crown Estate. This hereditary royal property, scattered over many areas including much of London's West End, was surrendered under George III to Parliament, and still is surrendered at the beginning of each new reign. In return, a Civil List was and is voted to cover the Crown's public expenses. Would it not be better they proposed, to do the surrendering the other way round?

Harold Wilson: "Instead of surrendering all that is

surrendered today and coming to Parliament for further increases, we could meet the Civil List increase by an agreed formula out of what has previously been surrendered, Crown money, and then surrender what is left to Parliament. It is as broad as it is long in the total provision and in total effect on the Treasury at the end of the day."

Lord Cobbold: "The only answer I can give is that that has not been considered."

That proposal, or something like it, will be reconsidered at the end of this study. Meanwhile Willie Hamilton, already extremely hostile to these suggestions, intervened to say that he preferred an annual review of "the facts" rather than at five- or ten-year intervals. As for the Crown Estate, he denied that it was "private property". Whereupon Lord Cobbold, probably scenting an unwelcome historical argument, tactfully replied: "I am afraid I am out of my depth there."*

On 6 July the Committee interviewed Douglas Allen, Permanent Secretary to the Treasury and official auditor of the Civil List, together with a Treasury accountant and Board of Revenue official. In this strictly financial section, Committee members and witnesses were allowed to have extracts from their own contributions removed from the minutes, if they wished, and replaced by asterisks before the Report was printed. There are asterisks in place of four paragraphs running (338–41), and many others.

Sir Douglas Allen began by stating: "As part of the Royal Prerogative, The Queen cannot be required to pay income tax unless Parliament specifically says so." A fortnight later

*The history of the Crown Estate is in Appendix 18 of the Report.

Boyd-Carpenter was questioning Mr W. A. Wood, secretary to the Crown Estate Commissioners. In answer to one of these questions, Wood projected for the Crown Estate "an annual increase of 7½ per cent in revenue". Boyd-Carpenter asked: "That is an increase in revenue, if my mathematics are right, which is improbable, of £300,000 a year?" Wood replied: "Yes, something of that order." A few minutes later, Hamilton saw another opportunity to attack the Crown Estate and to claim it for the people, not the Queen. "Mr Boyd-Carpenter's proposition", he said, "that the Crown Estate belongs of right to the Crown" was based upon "a myth". Boyd-Carpenter responded: "On a point of order, if Mr Hamilton is to be entitled to put to witnesses that views expressed by me are a myth, I might perhaps be allowed to put . . . the suggestion that Mr Hamilton's questions are based upon a nonsense." The Chairman cut in hastily: "I think on that happy note we might thank Mr Wood very much indeed" — and proceeded with the next witness.

This bit of scrapping between the extreme left and extreme right on the Committee seems to have released some other basic and widely differing feelings about the Queen and the royal finances. Douglas Houghton described how one day he found that fifty questions had been put down for him to answer about the Duchy of Lancaster, when he was its Chancellor. Many of them were from Hamilton. Houghton had promptly gone to the Queen and said: "I am proposing to answer identifiable questions in this way: 'I regret that in this matter I am answerable to the Crown and not to this House, and if there is a row about it I shall stand my ground.'" Carried away with enthusiasm, the Clerk to the Council of the Duchy and a witness, Mr E. R. Wheeler suddenly interjected: "Very good, Sir, very good, Sir, and we have lived by that ever since."

When they came to the Duchy's accounts, Hamilton thought that he was at last on to a good thing. For the pro-monarchists had to admit that the *privately* owned Duchy was forced to make its accounts *public*. Hamilton asked: "If it is a private estate, why are its accounts presented to Parliament?" Wheeler, seeing a chance to sidestep Hamilton, replied: "You will forgive me, I know, Sir, if I say I rather wish that the private side was emphasised more by them [the accounts] not being presented to Parliament. . . ." St John-Stevas, seeing the chance of a tease, added: "Perhaps we should change the law in this respect." To which Wheeler responded: "I would not be averse." St John-Stevas wickedly said: "I think this is possibly what Mr Hamilton is suggesting." But Hamilton objected, saying, "I should get it on record that I am violently opposed to that."

With the publication of the Report came two draft reports, one of which was rejected emphatically by the majority, the other rejected narrowly. Hamilton proposed to abolish the Civil List and to pay Her Majesty "the rate for the job", namely £100,000. Princess Anne's £6,000 was to be abolished. The annuity of the Queen Mother was to be no more than a prime minister's pension. Prince Philip's annuity was to be reduced to £20,000 and his household abolished. Princess Margaret's and the Duke of Gloucester's annuities were to cease. The younger sons of the Monarch were to receive nothing. The Queen could pay necessary annuities out of her £100,000. All royal income was to be taxed. And there would be a Select Committee on royal expenditure every five years. (This would ensure that her expenditure was never *not* under discussion — and this, of course, was Hamilton's intention.) His proposals were defeated by three votes to nine.

Houghton also proposed to abolish the Civil List, but it would be replaced by a Crown Commission, the Monarchy having been transformed into a Department of State. The Queen would become a kind of super civil servant, and all her expenses would be looked after by other civil servants, supervised by Parliament. One result of these proposals would no doubt have been a much cheaper but also less efficient entourage for Britain's Head of State. As things were, the Court was very tightly run, with a good deal of voluntary service on great occasions. This would all have been swept away, leaving the Queen as Head of State and nothing more. Would she have been able to infuse magic into such a set-up? If she did, it would only have been the most powerful magic that enabled her to do so. The proposal, though popular on the left, was defeated by seven votes to eight.

Despite all the suggestions for reform of the royal finances, the result was quite different. The Civil List was simply increased, as the Queen had requested in her "Gracious Message", from £475,000 to £980,000. The Government would surely have felt distinctly ungracious if it had offered anything less, considering that the Civil List had already been in deficit for ten years — a deficit that was being met out of the Queen's privy purse (private resources). At least the royal finances were no longer in the red. And they had been discussed from many angles, the Report being published, as already noted, for the first time.

It is now necessary to make a brief review of the royal tax situation at the beginning of 1992, in order to assess the coming changes.

On 24 July 1990, Margaret Thatcher, the Prime Minister, announced in Parliament that Her Majesty's Civil List would be fixed at about £7.9 million per year for the next ten-year period, instead of a supplement, if required, being voted annually. Should there be a surplus, it would be brought forward into the next ten-year period.

One press article characteristically predicted that any surplus, due to falling inflation, would be pocketed on the Queen's behalf by her advisers.

The Opposition leader Neil Kinnock, welcomed the change as promoting efficiency through forward planning. He also welcomed the Royal Household's change to professional management consultants for the same reason. However, Tony Benn and Dennis Skinner, both left-wingers, denounced the sums paid to the Royal Family, Skinner including in the "handout", as he called it, "all the hangers-on at the Palace". Antony Beaumont-Dark (Conservative) welcomed the ten-year period, but thought that it would be "proper, just and laudable" to tax the Sovereign; while Ron Brown (Labour) asked, "Who elected the Royal Family? . . . Why should they get a penny?"

Our next stage must be to look at some of the opinions that have been expressed on royal taxes since 1972, both in books and interviews.

Beginning with written opinions, the first point to notice is the total lack of urgency in almost all attitudes to the subject. For example, four popular and successful publications of the 1970s and 1980s show no interest whatever in the Civil List.* Of three books whose authors discuss it, *The Enchanted Glass: Britain and its Monarchy*, by Tom Nairn, cites two arguments against a monarchy — cost and snobbery — and two generally advanced in favour — it saves us from dictatorship and costs less than a president. Philip Howard's *British Monarchy* analyses the Civil List dispassionately for four pages and very tentatively suggests a change: "It may be what needs a little pruning is the royal finances, expecially the exemption from tax." Brian Hoey in a BBC book, *Monarchy*, goes meticulously through the Civil List without criticising it. His most interesting piece of information pictures a contented Royal Household and generous Queen: there have been no strikes at Buckingham Palace "as yet" — the staff having been under the Civil Service Union since 1946. Lastly, Theo Aronson, a writer who has known well a member of the Royal Family, Princess Alice of Athlone, tackles the taxation question in his *Monarchy in Transition* by implication rather than assertion. "Pride in the Monarchy", he writes, "increases as the economic power of Britain diminishes"; the implication being that people are unlikely to remove a royal prerogative and suddenly start taxing the chief traditional source of national pride and glamour.

It was early in 1992, shortly before the Government's new era for royal finances began on 1 April, that Philip Hall launched his expert republican attack. There had been ominous tax rumbles throughout 1991, but things were

The Queen Observed, a compendium edited by Trevor Grove; *The Queen Mother* by Anne Morrow; Princess Alice's *Memoirs*; and *A Guide to Political Institutions*, by Hanson and Walles, in which ten pages are allotted to the Monarchy.

never the same again on the tax front after the Hall onslaught; for one thing, it was given the full treatment, in the press and by the media. Hall's weapon was his book, *Royal Fortune*, which had long been brewing and which accused the Monarchy of "tax avoidance" (not, of course, "tax evasion", which is a criminal offence). A review of *Royal Fortune* in The *Economist*, of which the Palace approved, made a strong point against Hall's argument that the Queen ought to pay income tax: "it could be the thin end of an awkward wedge". Her financial advisers would be bound to propose "some degree of tax planning, but how could the most elementary piece of tax avoidance be reconciled with the dignity of the Monarchy? The imposition of income tax", argued the defenders of the Queen's tax exemption, "could actually aggravate political sensitivities over the royal finances."

It all depends, summed up The *Economist*'s reviewer, on how big are the Queen's private assets: "Sunday newspaper stories estimating her 'wealth' at 'around £7 billion' conjure up a fabulously rich monarch. . . . The picture is misleading." To cut a long review short, it reckoned that "the yield to the Treasury in royal income tax would be about £2 million at most".

One almost hopes that this picture is equally "misleading", otherwise there will inevitably be a future "bicycling monarchy" for a country that still seems to prefer a "Rolls-Royce" one. A bicycling or even a jogging monarchy will be the only one that the family can afford.

Passing from written to spoken opinion, all the interviews on royal taxation were conducted several years after the above books were written. In consequence they partook of the "crisis" atmosphere of 1992 in no longer being detached and leisurely in tone — but they were no more unanimous. Those who knew the Queen or Royal Family personally were naturally against creating a "cheap" monarchy through punitive taxation. Martin Charteris, the Queen's former very successful private secretary, was anxious that the taxation enthusiasts should realise exactly what they were recommending. It's no good, he thought, trying to convert the critics with the old arguments against royal income tax: "that all taxes are raised in the Queen's name and so she cannot very well tax herself; and that she has already made her contribution by surrendering the Crown Estate". Instead, let them consider the effects on the Queen's life, if taxed. Might she have to give up Balmoral? Her life-style is very important, and there would be a danger of reducing the British to a Scandinavian monarchy, which suits them but would have no point here. Charteris summed up with: "'Don't shoot Father Christmas', as they say; don't prune the Royal Family with too sharp a knife."

Another friend of the Royal Family agreed with critics that a hereditary monarchy is expensive, but worth it.

Nigel Dempster and Douglas Keay, writers on royalty, were both pessimistic. Young people, said Dempster, living on council estates, call the Civil List "our money" and want to keep it for themselves; while Keay believed the taxation issue was "very serious indeed". In contrast, Hugo Vickers took what might be called the traditional line on any sudden panic: "The Queen should do nothing about the taxation rumpus. It will pass."

And so it might have already, but for an unusually extended series of contributions to the royal "rompos", as Prince Albert would have called it, by the family's own younger members. It is time to recall the truly sensational events of the summer of 1992, a summer of wintry discontent for the Monarchy, lit up by occasional flashes of an all-too Mediterranean sun and raked by the over-long lens of a paparazzo's camera.

CHAPTER
THREE

The Young Royals

**"I think this is what the young members find difficult —
the regimented side."**

Her Majesty Elizabeth II in the film Elizabeth R

Nineteen ninety-two was the Year of the Young Royals. Not that our parents would ever have heard of a creature called a "Young Royal". But today the people — the ones who make and change language — have adopted the title "Young Royals" quite firmly, and that is what they must be.

Because the Year of the Young Royals was not a good one, it may be an idea to begin by remembering one of the species who describes herself as blissfully happy because she has broken the mould. Clearly if every unhappy young royal decided on self-exile from the clan, the clan itself would peter out. So, while the thirty year olds are trying — or not trying — rather wretchedly to make the thing work, a twenty-seven year old has opted out.

Mrs Marina Mowatt, only daughter of Princess Alexandra and Sir Angus Ogilvy, married Paul, the man she loved, on 2 February 1990, but not before their baby was well on the way. Marina, of course, was well placed to step out of the semi-gilded cage. Her position being twenty-sixth place from the throne, she was doing no possible damage to the Monarchy by reverting to normal. Indeed, the passage of time will probably show us many more semi-royals following Marina's example, even if it will no longer be necessary to make a symbolic stand for independence by reversing the normal order of marriage and baby.

Naturally there will be endless different ways in which the hybrid royals can enter the real world. The pleasantest way from the point of view of their parents would obviously be the one chosen by Lady Helen Windsor, daughter of the Duke and Duchess of Kent. Looking over one shoulder at her grandmother, Princess Marina of Greece, and her great-grandfather, King George V, Helen got married to Tim Taylor on 18 July 1992 in the royal chapel of St George's, Windsor, beneath the very same carved closet (like a box at the theatre) from which her forebear, Queen Victoria, watched the wedding of her eldest son. But over the other shoulder the bride saw the wide stream of real life flow invitingly by.

Princess Margaret had to take a pronounced step to make sure of her own children looking the right way. Long before they were grown up she made it clear that neither her son nor her daughter would lead the life of young royals, even though they had a king and queen for grandparents. She was wholly successful. Few would want to argue that there is no give-and-take, no resilience left in this modern Monarchy. The complications come not with the Monarch's sister and daughter and their children, but with the Monarch's sons. Their wives are the mothers of the immediate heirs to the throne.

It is fair to say that but for a blatantly intrusive press, the younger members of the Royal Family would never have found themselves in the dock. There would have been alarm, perhaps, over the Duchess of York's divorce, but not shock changing into pruriency. A divorce for the Princess of Wales might not even have been mentioned. However, shocked and embarrassed, sections of the public began demanding an end to our "free press", but this was only after the great summer build-up of hostile public reaction, unwittingly assisted, it must be said, by people as far away from the centre of the royal circle as David Mellor and Antonia de Sancha. By the autumn of 1992 the media had implanted three shifting images of mild pornography in a bemused public mind. A blurred photograph that the *Sun* had called "going toe far" might have been captioned Antonia or Fergie or Madonna.

The soft porn of Summer 1992 will already have slipped, one hopes, from the forefront of the public mind. Is it right to recall it as time recedes? Yet without some such recapitulation, a book on the future of the Monarchy would be impossible. After some doubts, it has finally seemed to me that a major question about the Monarchy can be squarely faced only by sacrificing to some extent the minor virtue of reticence.

At least one advantage can be gained for the Royal Family from an analysis of Andrew Morton's poisoned chalice, *Diana: Her True Story*, though this is only a beginning. It is possible to contradict several waspish lies that have attempted to sting the country's future King. For instance, odious suggestions that the Prince of Wales showed no concern for his son, Prince William, when the child was accidentally hit on the head at school with a golf club.

Morton's story was a travesty of the truth: that Charles went blithely off to the opera with friends just when seven-year-old William was about to undergo surgery. The facts were that the anxious father stayed with his son in hospital until the surgeon assured him that all would be well and there was absolutely nothing more he could do. After leaving his private secretary with orders to let him know immediately if there was any untoward development (which, of course, there was not), Prince Charles arrived at the opera just in time to meet a group from Europe who had come over especially to see him.

Apart from typical incidents from Morton's book like the above, the overall message was that the Prince of Wales's marriage was in dire trouble. This is the moment for a first glance at the man who would have to cope with this situation, while carrying out his duties as heir to the throne. What sort of Prince of Wales did the country really possess? For the future of the Monarchy in the twenty-first century would largely depend on him.

Only one thing was missing from the make-up of Prince Charles when he grew up: a dash of comforting ordinariness. In fact, his character and talents have always demonstrated an *embarras des richesses.* His friends like to call him a "Renaissance Prince". If necessary, he could have succeeded in more than one of the professions. He was already trained in the fighting services, as all royal princes are, and he could have turned with success to teaching (he is a good speaker and likes explaining things) or medicine, farming, forestry, architecture or another of the arts such as painting or music. His ancestor, King Edward VII, modestly admitted that he knew nothing about "ar-r-r-t" (with a rollicking r) but a good deal about "ar-r-rangement". The present Prince of Wales would consider the art of arrangement as scarcely worth spending time on, except perhaps to fill in an odd minute before lunch or dinner. Later on we shall have to see what it is that makes the Prince of Wales tick so relentlessly without a second of the normal idling that goes for activity, of day-dreaming that passes itself off in the normal world as thought. For the moment let us note one striking thing about this Prince. In his concern for new ranges of stimulating ideas he resembles Prince Albert more closely than any other of the Prince Consort's descendants.

Meanwhile, it is important to analyse the two speeches that the Prince of Wales has delivered in the House of Lords. The first was in June 1974, when he was twenty-six, and the second in June 1975. The subject of the first was "Sport and Leisure", of the second "Voluntary Service in the Community". Each of these subjects for debate made a special appeal to the young Prince, eliciting from him the same kind of revealing words and phrases. For instance, the problem of bringing derelict land into use for leisure activities could only be solved by "determination and impetus". The Government needed to develop "a central impetus" to encourage local authorities, while avoiding "bureaucratic control" and removing "the dead hand of boredom and frustration". The young, he predicted, would soon be capable of self-organisation.

In his second speech he recommended the peculiar merits of "adventure" as against "frustration", adding that once an "impetus" had been provided, it would be "developed by the young people themselves". With his energy and enthusiasm,

Charles is indeed a Prince of Wales for the young. Three other things emerged from an amalgamation of the two speeches:

That *planning* for leisure and youth services was vital — but it must be without red tape (a difficult combination).

That young people should learn to test themselves, just as young Charles was taught to do at Gordonstoun school.

That we British learnt too little from abroad, notably from Holland, about co-ordinating our leisure.

The Prince's *bêtes noires* and enthusiasms already stood out as clearly in his twenties as they do in his forties: down with bureaucracy and boredom; up with impetus.

Incidentally, in a recent television series on the Monarchy, James Whitaker said that the Prince of Wales "comes dangerously close to politics in his search for a role". I shall have more to say about the Prince's "role", but in regard to party politics, no one could fail to see, after reading his (so far) only two Parliamentary speeches, how different is his approach from that of all party politicians of the present day. His denunciations of bureaucracy would sound strange on the lips of a Labour politician, while his fervent belief in planning is alien to the Tories. In other words, he is neither an individualist (Tory) nor a collectivist (socialist). Of course you do find members of both Houses of Parliament who are non-partisan, but, in the last resort, their influence is exerted within the party machine. Compared with this, the Prince's contribution is positively disembodied: "impetus".

It might be thought that the Prince and Princess of Wales would have been drawn closely together by their common interest in suffering humanity. Diana's extraordinary gifts of empathy with the sick and unhappy are well understood and rightly admired, including her courage in being among the first to touch AIDS sufferers. Charles's work for the disadvantaged is perhaps less well known.

In an elegant cream, red and black leaflet entitled "Working Together" and signed by Charles, he demonstrates how seriously he has gone into all the ideas presented in it — mainly his own ideas. A "Caring Network" was set up by him and known by such plain-spoken names as "Business in the Community", "The Prince's Youth Business Trust" and half-a-dozen more. But it needs only one interpretive glance to realise that imagination — social imagination and sensitivity — forms an essential ingredient of the Prince's "Network". He does not refer to his "collection" or "group" of organisations, but to his *family* of organisations, thus indicating that they are all concerned with people. Some of them help the adventurous young and several of them help "disadvantaged young people". A coloured brochure illustrated by photographs of those who have been helped with grants, loans or training shows that one-fifth to one-sixth of the disadvantaged are black. Scotland and Wales have their own very active Trusts and all have their common objective: to assist not professions, not categories, not types, but "individuals and communities". It has been said of Mrs Robinson, the extremely popular Irish President: "She is involved in the small print of people's lives." The same thing might be said of Prince Charles.

Occasionally one hears criticisms of the Prince for his many alleged holidays in Scotland, or Italy, or again at his country seat, Highgrove in Gloucestershire. In fact, his eight Trusts keep him extremely busy wherever he is, and exercise takes up but a small fraction of his time. The special place that polo occupies in his life will be explained later.

He has built a new annexe at Highgrove to accommodate those who have come to see him and must wait for a thinning in the queue. Significantly, there is an entrance to the annexe for wheelchairs. Admittedly, from the front of his house the Prince does not have to look at wheelchairs, but at the glorious spire of Tetbury church. However, he does not get much time to look out of the window or stand and stare from the front doorstep on an ordinary working day. One of his private secretaries who has been seconded to his office from an extremely busy publishing career is amazed by the amount of work he does for the Trusts while in Scotland, and how relatively little time he spends on huntin', fishin' and shootin'.

With Princess Diana's star quality focused directly upon the terminally sick, the AIDS victims, the dying, there would seem to be every reason for crediting the royal couple with a similar outlook on public life and its duties: he for the disadvantaged young adults, she for the disadvantaged elderly and young children. Throw in Princess Anne for endangered children the world over, and you might expect to have reached a cosy harmonious corner inhabited by a younger Royal Family of united do-gooders. The situation has not, alas, developed like that.

Leaving aside Princess Anne, who is unique for enjoying huge popularity on the strength of nothing but hard work — no glamour except that of dedication and success — the Prince and Princess of Wales have shown an approach to their own vocations that has nothing whatever in common but basic humanity.

In the old days a very extraordinary person used to be called *rara avis*, a rare bird. Princess Diana is not just an exotic, but a bird of Paradise. Trailing plumes of glory as if from some other, more heightened existence, she comes to offer a gift of loveliness that most of the sick and dying she visits have never set eyes on before. As a result, she may make someone here and there feel almost well again:

Now if thou wouldst, when all have given him over,
From death to life thou mightst him yet recover.

Her pure classical profile is totally out of place in hospital wards and, therefore, totally welcome.

What should she do to present herself? Nothing whatever. Deep thought or bright ideas about her personal offering would be superfluous. Like every great star, her duty is to give herself to her adorers almost without spoken words. Just smiles, or tears. The sad people she meets will effectively "charge" her, as from some secret batteries, and re-charge her as often as is needed. Even so, in making this exhausting gift of her own personality, she may feel drained and may need re-charging again in some different way — dancing, pop music — at the end of the day.

We know something about this business of giving out and getting re-charged from Queen Elizabeth the Queen Mother — and no doubt every great public star could add to the picture. The Queen Mother, who has never lacked self-knowledge, described the process as she had observed it in herself, using the actual word "re-charge".

How does the Prince of Wales work it? By public re-charge or private re-think? Surely, the latter. He has been trained over the years to use his brain. What an extraordinary education he has had. Twice snatched away from school or university to test the educational water in a different continent or country (Australia, Wales), he nevertheless managed to secure a good honours degree at Cambridge, having learnt to discourse with the purest example of an academic politician, Rab Butler. Charles has since succeeded in diluting the academic flavour in some degree, learning to talk the language and think the thoughts of the businessmen on whom so many of his Trusts depend. But there is no visible mysterious interchange between the Prince and his audience, interspersed with smiles and tears. His disadvantaged young people simply say "brilliant", "great", while he shows them how to work a word processor.

There is evidence of all this in the leaflet that Prince Charles put out about himself and his work. For the back cover someone has taken a spontaneous, relaxed photograph of the Prince, as he passes through what appears to be a group of young people seeking help, or having received help, from one of his Trusts. The Prince's head is slightly bent and instead of facing the camera with a wide grin he has a quizzical, even puzzled smile — more quiz, in fact, than smile. That is the familiar and well-understood expression of Britain's future King. It expresses concern, modesty, good-nature, and seems to be asking, "Do you think this project is going to be too hard for us? I think you and I can manage it together."

March 1992 was the date when the approaching end of the Yorks' marriage was made public. They separated. Ultimately it was expected that they would divorce. (Mrs Susan Barrantes, the Duchess's mother, said the divorce would be in 1994.) At first the announcement of the separation had no very serious effects on the Monarchy. Nobody thought the collapse of this five-year marriage would wound anyone but the parties themselves and possibly the Queen (she is devoted to her grandchildren, Princess Beatrice and Princess Eugénie), though there were already two other vulnerable areas. The score between marriage and divorce in the Queen's family had now levelled out at two all. Moreover some of the Duchess's early post-separation actions showed an ominous insensitivity and incomprehension of royal trends in the 1990s. The public did not wish the young royals to set an example in luxurious living; elegance would be more to the general taste. A well-wisher told the Duchess that she had made a mistake in moving out of her expensive former home at Sunninghill Park, after the separation, into another luxury mansion, Romenda Lodge; she ought to have chosen something more reasonable. The public would not like such extravagance. At which the Duchess of York opened wide her uncomprehending blue eyes and asked the immortal question: "But don't they want me to be happy?"

For the rest, the Duchess of York seemed at first to fade back into semi-private life. Former attempts to build her up as Sarah Ferguson, a distinguished lady related to the Buccleuchs, were tacitly dropped and she became by common consent the more appropriate "Fergie". Everyone knew that Fergie had lived in Switzerland with a racing-driver before her marriage, so she was just moving on again. No one minded much, though the public were exceptionally fond of the Yorks' children. Only the ratpack knew (if it was not guesswork rather than knowledge) that Fergie and Diana had had a divorce pact. On 7 June 1992 the *Mail on*

Sunday used letters two inches high to report an alleged dual announcement by the Princess and the Duchess: "WE DIVORCE TOGETHER!" In smaller letters, beneath grim, wild portraits of the pair, came two captions: *"Backed Out*: Diana yesterday"; *"Went Ahead*: Duchess of York".

The Duchess of York was said to have felt let down when the Princess of Wales opted out of their divorce pact. "I will not leave my husband," the *Daily Mail* reported the Princess as saying on 10 June. "She has accepted", continued the *Mail,* "that her sense of duty and the welfare of her children demand that she must make a determined effort to repair her marriage."

If Diana was not living up to Fergie's hopes of her as a royal rebel, she had done enough to revolutionise the press for the whole summer — and we know now that the Princess of Wales was partly responsible for the sensation foreshadowed in the first week of June.

The major event was to be the serialisation in the *Sunday Times*, beginning on 7 June. It may have been in large part the "true story" of Diana, but it was certainly not the true story of her husband. Even if the marriage had become unhappy after the birth of Prince Harry, there were plenty of valid reasons why this should be so without dragging in the family character of the Prince of Wales. For instance, Morton stated that the Prince quarrelled with his mother, the Queen, over her Christmas message to the nation and Commonwealth. The implication was that he had been taken aback by the Queen's promise to continue "for some years to come" in her service as Monarch, instead of abdicating in his favour. This caused such princely "anger", wrote Morton, "that he refused to speak to his mother for several days".

That is rubbish. It is well known that the Queen never discusses abdication because it is not on the cards. Abdication has a bad name in Britain, whereas venerable queens become more and more popular. Nor would his mother's approaching abdication, if it were indeed on the way, have suited Prince Charles's own plans. We shall see in due course that the Prince's very specific preparations for his kingship do not involve his mother's premature departure.

During that week of pre-serialisation there were signs of frenzied press activity in other papers besides the *Sunday Times*. On Saturday 6 June, the *Daily Mail* printed a double spread on another book about the Princess, to be published in New York the following month: *Diana, A Princess and Her Troubled Marriage*, by Lady Colin Campbell. Banner headlines declared the unfortunate Diana to have been "GORGING ON CUSTARD AND CAKE" — a victim of bulimia nervosa, the anorexic disease that makes the victim resort to vomiting and even suicide. We were told by the *Mail*'s medical correspondent, a lady with the comforting name of Hope, that the chief symptom of bulimia is "an exaggerated fear of fatness". Its roots lie partly in "the modern preoccupation with body image, but also in trying to deal with stress".

Which came first in the Princess? The bulimia or the stress? Since neither bulimia nor anorexia is uncommon in young girls, and since Diana and her elder sister Sarah each had one of these diseases, it seems likely that the stress in the Princess's marriage was partly the result of her precondition, particularly as it began during her engagement. That, in fact, is what the Queen believes.

Yet one more preliminary article — this time in the

Spectator — came out just before the crucial 7 June. Henry Porter covered over two pages with fascinating fill-in details about the coming serial. His points can be summarised:

The *Sunday Times* paid Morton at least £240,000.

The Royal Family would not defend themselves.

Except for the final stage of cut-throat competition, the ratpack hunt together, making themselves a formidable power.

Their sources are Palace moles, generally "at servant level", or detectives.

The ratpack suffer from the Malvolio complex, convinced that members of the Royal Family are in love with them.

They range from monarchists (James Whitaker) to republicans (Andrew Morton).

At last the long-awaited Sunday arrived. The first extraordinary thing to notice was that the worst of all the Princess's five "suicide" attempts occurred over ten years before, even before Prince William was born. Six months' pregnant and suffering cruelly from morning sickness, the Princess had apparently thrown herself down a wooden staircase at Sandringham. The Queen Mother was the first person to see the seemingly lifeless bundle land in a heap at the bottom. Later in the book the Princess was to describe her self-inflicted cuts and bruises as "cries for help" rather than genuine suicide attempts. Yet the main headlines in the *Sunday Times*, introducing the Morton article ran: "Diana driven to five suicide bids by 'uncaring' Charles" — uncaring, it was suggested, because of his overriding friendship with Camilla Parker Bowles. Eventually Diana was cured by the persuasions of her best friend, Carolyn Bartholomew, to see a doctor. This, then, is the second extraordinary thing. Much of the worst was over *before* Morton wrote his book. Many people hoped that the book had actually given the Royal Family strength by bringing the bulimia into the open and so putting the Princess on the path to recovery. That was not so. For the Elizabethan-style melodrama (Amy Robsart may have given a cry for help, too, when she fell downstairs at Cumnor) was too late to help Diana — she had already recovered — but in good time to damage the Royal Family, particularly Prince Charles.

It was the publication of Morton's actual book on 16 June that made clear how much he owed to Princess Diana's "friends" — and, we now know, to the Princess herself. Thanking them effusively in the Acknowledgements, he specifically stressed their "laying aside the ingrained habits of discretion and loyalty which proximity to royalty invariably engenders".

Not to be outdone, the *Sunday Times* must have decided to attribute Diana's sad story not so much to her friends as to herself: "Diana: Her Own Story", it announced on the first day. Without making too much of mere captions, it is impossible to overlook the innuendo here: her friends were the intermediaries, she herself was the source. Why else did she not contradict the ungenerous picture painted of the Royal Family? The much publicised photograph of the Princess greeting her friend, Mrs Bartholomew, warmly at the entrance to the Bartholomew home after the serialisation began was taken with the co-operation of the Princess's "minders" (detectives). Normally they do everything to keep the press as far away as possible. On this occasion they made way for the cameras. The claim that the book would in fact strengthen the Royal Family by telling the truth was false. The book had the effect of lowering everyone all round. To reveal the attempted suicides by the young mother of two schoolchildren was inexcusable.

The *Mail on Sunday* weighed in as usual, this time with a clever ironic caption under a smiling photograph of Diana: "Public Face: The Princess hides her secret heartache." From then on the press flooded in with prophecies and queries ("It's all over." "Can they divorce?") despite Sir Richard Luce, the Vice-Chancellor of Buckingham University, having pronounced doom on the *Sunday Times* through the columns of its sister paper: "To the Editor of *The Times*. Sir, I will no longer buy the *Sunday Times*. I hope many others will do the same." Two things, he thought, were certain: the nation would show its "revulsion for the vultures", and pray that the Prince and Princess would still "set an example" in marriage. Neither certainty has been fulfilled. All through June the vultures came in flocks rather than as single spies, though July was to see some more diversified skirmishing, in the sense that the *Sunday Times* leapt to its own defence. However, before leaving Diana's "True" or "Own" story, it is necessary to note a few of the points that have virtually escaped the interest of the vultures.

One of the Princess's complaints concerned her cluelessness as a young, untutored, royal wife. "Nobody taught me a single thing," she was reported as saying. But this ignorance did not stop her from trying to find the information she needed elsewhere. If the Church did not counsel her, she could and did find her counselling in the philosophy of reincarnation. "The spirits will look after me," was her touching hope.* When she had had dreams during pregnancy of sea monsters, her husband took it seriously and put her on to a classical interpretive therapist. The Princess was not after that sort of thing at all. She discovered the fortune-tellers, the clairvoyants, the readers of tarot cards. Within herself all sorts of intuitions began developing: that she would never be Queen, that there would be no King Charles III. At first many monarchists were shattered by these revelations about royal guidance, until we remembered that since time immemorial people have examined the entrails of birds or other omens before making a speech or fighting a battle. The ancient Romans did it; the Sloane Rangers and many others, including Nancy Reagan, did it.

Nor must the isolation of the Princess be exaggerated. Apparently we should be wrong to think of her as alone with her psychotherapists, her physiotherapists, her fortune-tellers and her "friends". Her only brother, Charles Spencer, has given a much more reassuring picture. He himself and his three sisters, Sarah, Jane and Diana, make "a very strong combination" because of their parents' divorce. "As a brother", he adds, "I feel it's my duty to remind her [Diana] that she is adored and that she does do an exceptional amount of good for an awful lot of people."†

I must now return for the last time to my main grievance against Morton's story. He says: "The story

*On 19 December 1992 it was reported to the *Mirror* by one of the Princess's spiritual counsellors that the spirit of Earl Spencer, Diana's late father, had appeared at a seance (though Diana could not see him) and apologised for leaving her when she needed him.

†*Hello!*, 10 October 1992. After the Prince and Princess's separation, Diana spent Christmas 1992 with her brother at Althorp.

of [the Princess's] transformation from victim to victor is the subject of this book." He publishes a catalogue of humiliation, disgust and wretchedness from the past — but not the dead past. It could only do harm to those who are in the thick of it and cause pain to those on the fringes, the very old and very young, the Queen Mother and the two young Princes. Morton describes the Princess of Wales as having become a victor instead of a victim. Over whom? He does not say. But over the Royal Family is the implied answer. One thing is certain. Morton's book and its serialisation provided some of the prerequisites for the subsequent royal separation: exposure, partisanship and relentless publicity.

A few remarkable strands emerged as the weeks of summer passed. Perhaps the most striking of all was the attitude of the Palace. There was no public attitude, just a virtual silence. Without the help of the "friends and footmen" class, the press would scarcely have been able to quote the Palace at all. No doubt that was the idea.

At the same time the press, in Penny Junor's perceptive words, "began to become part of the story". This was all wrong, because its correct role is to observe and report, not to take part in the action. Yet here were the rivals, the *Mirror* and the *Sun*, dramatising their own house of cards (for circulation appears to be a house of cards) far more effectively than the House of Windsor. What we had learnt to recognise as a "cry for help" on the lips of the Princess of Wales had become a "cry for attention" in the pages of the tabloids (*Guardian*). One paper had the brilliantly imaginative thought of pitting the Princess of Wales against her sister, Lady Jane Fellowes, who is married to the Queen's private secretary. No one fell for it.

With the press part of the story, the newspapers began shredding each other. *Private Eye* launched into its own version of the *Funday Times* with the headlines, "Grave Constitutional Crisis Rocks Fairyland Over Funday Times Revelations", followed by "Grimm Stuff. Said one who used to share a pumpkin with the Princess, 'She used to be a fun-loving girl . . . but now she sits sadly in her turret, spinning a yarn which only the Funday Times is stupid enough to print in full'." In a panel given over to "A Doctor", you are told that if you feel sick, "you are almost certainly a victim of Bullshitia Murdocha, or 'reading the papers', as it is more commonly known . . . If you think you are suffering from bullshitia murdocha you should contact Andrew Neil [the editor of the *Sunday Times*] immediately and be sick all over him."

Two weeks later Andrew Knight, Chairman of News International of which Rupert Murdoch was owner, along with the *Sunday Times*, picked up the gage and hurled it at David English and the *Daily Mail*. Knight chose the *Spectator* as his platform from which to pillory those who had denounced Murdoch and his "servile republican editor", Neil. Did not Sir David English bid £200,000 at the auction for Morton's book, wrote Knight, only to be beaten by the *Sunday Times*? Why should the Murdoch bid be seen as part of a republican conspiracy to defeat the Monarchy? Had the *Mail* had some supposedly loyal motive in bidding? So far, so fair. But then Knight went on to argue that institutions like the Monarchy can survive because they are adaptable ("they constantly adapt"), the inference being that a marriage cannot adapt and therefore may be exposed as finished.

Yet marriage is also an institution. Marriages constantly adapt and should not have their life support taken away from them by ruthless publicity until they are quite dead. And their life support is privacy.

However, in the third week of August the royal scene was to move away, temporarily, from Diana to the York front; from words to action.

Twenty-two topless photographs in colour showed the Duchess of York sunbathing, embracing and generally disporting herself in the grounds of a villa near St Tropez, in the South of France, with John Bryan, her financial adviser and a Texan friend. Also with her were her two daughters, Beatrice and Eugénie, and her detectives. The *Daily Mirror*, victor this time in the new battle of circulation, achieved ten pages of pictures on the first day, though the *Standard* that same evening photographed the *Mirror*'s front page on its own front page, accompanied by the caption: "She's topless and they're kissing . . . scandalous pictures of Fergie and her friend bring Royal Family crisis." The *Sun*, furious at being out-disgraced by a fellow tabloid, relied on verbal wit to restore the balance. "PHOTOE" ran the enigmatic code, to be explained as "Toe-sucking John Bryan last night failed to get a ban slapped on pictures of topless Fergie". Next day the *Sun* had some more wit — "Fergie's last boob" — and a photograph. The *Daily Mail* had the best joke, by cartoonist "mac", a joke that was to be made a thousand times before the press were done with "Fergie and Johnny". An elderly couple are plodding home with shopping bags, stick and junior. A young couple is lying entwined beside the path.

"Look, Grandma," points the child, "there's a girl over there getting financial advice."

There was something in the Duchess's situation to annoy absolutely everybody. Not surprisingly the Queen was in "acute dismay". She and Prince Philip have never liked intrusive lenses, since one poked up through a distant table at their honeymoon restaurant in Paris; and now the distances and power have multiplied. If the Queen and her Consort discussed with longing the present French system of legal privacy, it would have been entirely understandable.*

Taxpayers were angry because they had to pay for the detectives to watch the delectable poolside scene, and many others were shocked by the presence at this bacchanalia of two small children. Those who approved of toplessness could not help remembering that places like St Tropez itself and, indeed, most other public French beaches could have harboured Fergie topless and no one would have been any the wiser. It was the private pool that excited the paparazzi. The largest group of all deplored such senseless *antics*, choosing a word that stood for stupidity rather than vice, though both were totally inappropriate in a "royal". Finally, so distraught was the Duchess's mother, who happened to hear the news on holiday in Biarritz, that she told the press she knew the whole thing was laid on by "spies".

A MORI poll on 22 August showed the public's sympathies now almost equally divided over press intrusion into royal privacy. The events of the summer of 1992 were responsible for diminished royal sympathy compared with two years

---

*However, French fines are generally very low, often no more than £1,000, and are regarded as "a licence to breach". The sum of £60,000 granted by a French court to the Duchess of York was exceptional.

earlier. That suggested a difficult period ahead for the Royal Family. "The crime of Sarah Ferguson and Princess Diana", wrote Janet Watts in the *Observer*, "is to be ordinary young women catapulted into the extraordinariness of royal life for which they received neither help nor training."

Suddenly the *Sun* bounced back into the lead, determined to wipe out its humiliation. Not only had the *Mirror* stolen a march over the St Tropez *frolic* (another favourite word of those wishing not to be too censorious), but now a mobile telephone conversation between the Princess of Wales and her friend, James Gilbey, had stolen a march in the United States. The transcript of the tapes had already been published by the *Enquirer*, a supermarket tabloid; and, on 23 August, it was to appear in the *Sunday Express*. News International (the *Sun*) had been sitting on these very tapes for two years. Now, at last, on Monday 24 August, the *Sun* gave the tapes a five-page spread and, on the Tuesday, issued an invitation to "Listen to Di tapes on phone" — at 36p a minute, cheap rate, for half an hour. The tapes were named by the *Sun*, "Dianagate".

They turned out to be no "Dianagate", in the sense of revealing the betrayal of the Prince by Diana with a lover. James Gilbey had been Diana's friend since before her marriage. In 1989, on the mobile telephone, he was calling her "Squidgy" and "Darling" as he always had, trying to encourage her when she poured out her woes. He would whisper down the telephone, "I love you, love you, love you." This tape may even have been one of her last big wails before she reached the stable "plateau" that her brother was to talk about in the Morton book. As for the subjects of her woe, they ranged from the relatively mild to the unbearable, centring on three things: her supposed exclusion from the Royal Family circle, the Queen Mother's having looked at her strangely and Prince Charles's having made her life "torture".

And who tapped the telephone? Cyril Reenan, a retired bank manager who picked up the "Dianagate" conversation with his powerful radio scanner, seems to have been punished enough by an enormous hate mail. "I didn't know what to do with it," said Reenan after the *Sun* had acquired the tape from him. "I was stuck with it and I was frightened of it."*

Four days after the "Dianagate" tape was published, a "Fergiegate" tape was offered to the *Sun*. A dialogue between the Yorks of January 1990, it had remained in another radio buff's possession until radio-osmosis drew it forth from a drawer and into the *Sun*'s office. Then at last the brilliant yet simple idea that no one had hitherto thought of struck the *Sun*. It handed the tape over to Sir Matthew Farrer, the Queen's lawyer.

By the first week in September the *Sun* had gone behind the clouds again. Its "Dianagate" tapes were banned by Sir Louis Blom-Cooper, Chairman of the Independent Committee for the Supervision of Telephone Information Services, who drew special attention to the very different effect of *listening* to a private conversation and *reading* it in a newspaper. The tape gave you "all the silences, the stresses, the emotional content".

*Since Reenan's actions, it has been suggested that the Security Services may have tapped the telephone conversation and deliberately broadcast it a few days after it had taken place. The same goes for the picking up of the other two tapes, "Camillagate" and "Fergiegate".

On the same day, 3 September, that Blom-Cooper banned the *Sun*'s so-called "love tape", Major James Hewitt, another of the Princess's confidants who once taught her riding and whose relations with her were questioned by the *Sun*, brought a libel action against News Group Newspapers.

There were now many conflicting thoughts about royalty jostling for acceptance in the late summer. In any pub, you would find that all the contradictory opinions had anger in common — anger that at a time when people were losing their jobs and homes, the rich should still be dealing in millions. "It's said the Queen is to give £4 million to Fergie." "They had better get off the front pages or there'll be a revolution by autumn." "But the Royal Family isn't whiter than white any more, so why shouldn't Fergie get what she can out of it? Sell the story for £10 million." "The press are a disgrace for printing it . . ." "We love you, Di" was still the cry of those the Princess visited in hospital wards, but a Cambridge don had suddenly lost patience with her. Did she, after all, understand loyalty? asked John Casey. "If she chooses to subvert the throne from within, encouraged by her moronic friends, then however good she may be in smelling suffering a mile off, and however many lives she may have gone through before the present one, there is one incarnation that I hope will never be hers — Queen of England."

When an opinion poll on the Royal Family came out a month later, the Queen came top and the Duchess of York bottom. Yet the Queen cannot again be completely at ease on her well-deserved eminence until changes are made. For the young royals, the Sarahs and Dianas of the future, guidance and counselling are their first necessities. Unless you are born to the job — which fewer and fewer people are — it is impossible to serve merely by the light of nature something as "curious" (Charles's word) as the Monarchy.

It is widely believed that on the more personal front the Queen persuaded the Prince and Princess of Wales to devote at least the next six months to mending their marriage. This alleged "council of peace" was said to have taken place after the Garter Ceremony at Windsor Castle in mid-June, which both the Prince and Princess attended. That should have brought the period of truce and rebuilding to the end of the year. And, indeed, the couple did embark on a joint visit to the Far East early in November. Alas, the press photographs of husband and wife in Seoul together only demonstrated how far they were apart. In any case a few days after Seoul, a second tape-bomb was to explode, this time in the *Daily Mirror*. As we shall see, it would succeed in devastating whatever hopes of peace and reconciliation the public may still have been keeping alive.

CHAPTER
FOUR

How the Royal Family See Themselves

I don't know about change. I have just tried to develop my side in ways that seemed appropriate . . . to struggle away at different schools, universities, Australia and Wales. As a result of that, trying to be relevant, which is what matters.

HRH The Prince of Wales, in an interview, September 1992

The Monarchy is a venerable institution whose outward and visible form is the Royal Family. The Greek word *monarch* means "one ruler", and that single ruler is drawn from a family whose right to be called "royal" is hereditary. So we always know in advance who are going to be the institution's most important members. Yet the Royal Family and the institution it embodies are far from being institutionalised.

Members of other institutions, which may be as different from each other as the European Community, the local Women's Institute or one of the older universities, are all kept together because they abide by the rules. If member states of the EC disagree with the rules, they can try to change them or get out. Members of the Royal Family can get out, as Edward VIII did, but he never fully understood which rule about royal marriage he was breaking because there are no rules. At the same time new members can join, by marriage. But marriage itself will remain the only initiation ceremony There is no training in dos and don'ts of a general kind, no structured picture of how it works, of where there is room for developments, or how best this or that newcomer might fit in.

Some people have begun to think that the whole royal institution is altogether too informal and loosely knit for modern times. A senior member of the family believes that there should be more long-term planning. But this would work best if there were some authority like an "elder statesman" to draw up the plans and see them carried out. As we have seen, Lord Mountbatten might have been that person — one of the very many reasons why his death was such a tragedy.

It might be thought that the already experienced Palace staff were the ones to organise the necessary advances in cohesion. They would certainly not be incapable of doing it. Nor would they be a danger from the angle of overdoing the regimentation. Today the Royal Household is moving in the direction of more informality rather than less. The Queen herself will sometimes take her private secretary, Sir Robert Fellowes, by surprise with the extent of her ability to dispense with petty ceremony. The same tendency to eliminate trivial regulations permeates every aspect of Palace life. Some years ago when I myself was calling at the Palace for information connected with an earlier book, I was fetched from an ante-room by a footman, according to protocol, and taken by him along the broad upstairs passages until we reached the official door, where I was deposited. When I arrived last summer to discuss this book, the procedure was much jollier. Charles Anson, the Queen's press secretary, fetched me direct from the ante-chamber; there were no intervening stages of protocol.

There is no reason why more long-term planning and less formal methods should not coexist in a modern monarchy. There could be a perfectly coherent "inside view" — by which I mean the Royal Family's own view — of the Monarchy's future which actually included a more relaxed approach to bringing it about. Meanwhile, in so far as there already exists any recognisable "inside view", it seems to resolve itself at present into four major areas of agreement.

The first centres on the Monarchy's overriding value — an absolute value for which can be offered untiring service and, indeed, sacrifice. The second area of agreement concerns the setting of "example". Unless the Royal Family are seen to be a good model, they will not achieve anything and will crumble, taking the whole monarchical system with them. Third, the media, one way or another, are making it impossible for the Monarchy to deal with and absorb its normal ration of human failings — let alone the hot geysers that now and then gush up from all institutions. Many royalists believe that the hounding of the Yorks by the press actually caused their divorce. Fourth, there is a spiritual dimension to the Monarchy that cannot be excluded from any assessment of its future.

However, before illustrating this fourfold "inside view" from the words of the Royal Family, I must enter one caveat. How can we be sure that even this relatively tentative presentation of royal opinion is true?

The truth is that we cannot be sure. Unless "royal opinion" is strictly limited to what we have heard the Queen saying on the television screen, or to what we have read under the signature of Prince Charles, we can never be certain that an alleged verbatim report is not a verbatim invention. A supposed statement by a member of the Royal Family might not be contradicted. That does not mean it must be accepted. There are other reasons for letting it run beside the possible fact that it is true — reasons which will be discussed later — but here and now it is necessary to issue a warning.

There was a jubilant evening when the fortieth anniversary of the Queen's reign was celebrated in her presence by her family, friends and well-wishers at Earls Court, with ballet, orchestra and song. The press as a whole warmly welcomed the group of cheerful faces in the royal box, the *Sun*, for instance, publishing a sparkling portrait of Princess Diana flashing smiles all around while Prince Charles, picking up one of them, returned an entirely unquizzical grin.

On second thoughts, however, this did not seem to satisfy the *Sun*. Where was the "royal rift" that, after all, is the best circulation booster known to modern editors? If Charles and Diana were not to be the estranged pair, another must be found. So a *Sun* reporter obliged with an account of a new "royal rift" that was intended to compare with the Waleses' troubles as Chernobyl would compare with a small IRA bomb. Printed immediately beneath its graceful photographs of the celebrating Royal Family, the caption ran: "Queen and Charles hide their growing feud at tribute show". We were told that "a simmering row which threatens the future of the Monarchy" was developing between two "stubborn" characters who would not give way to each other: the Queen refusing ever to abdicate; Charles to discuss his marriage, attend to the "boring papers" inside his red boxes or give up skiing after the Klosters tragedy.

There was nothing here that was either new or true, one might think. Nevertheless, the last paragraphs came in with a crash of double doom:

> It is a crisis which could not have come at a worse time for the Royal Family. They are already in turmoil.
> *Unless this rift is healed soon it could prove to be the straw that broke the camel's back.**

One hopes that such reporting sent the *Sun* yet again behind clouds of shame and derision. To choose an occasion that the *Sun* itself described as "all smiles" for its tocsin blast shows a rare combination of malice and mischief.

The *Daily Express* ran a similar story, but to do the editor justice, after a Palace protest, he arranged for a balancing article to be published in his paper two days later. Among the many errors which required correcting was reference to "the Balmoral conference . . . famous throughout royal circles". These conferences do not exist and are a persistent media myth, as any real "insider" knows.

Again, it was said that "the Prince snubbed his mother at Balmoral. For most of August he was at Craigowan Lodge." In fact, the Prince did not spend even one night at Craigowan Lodge in summer 1992. In August he spent a total of fifteen nights at Balmoral, as a guest of the Queen. Once more a media myth persists due to use of a cuttings library.

*   *   *

*Robert Jobson, royal reporter, *Sun*, 27 October 1992.

A study of the Royal Family's own view of its future may perhaps seem at first sight naïvely wholesome, but the Monarchy is an ideal as well as an institution. And ideals are always likely to sound naïve when they do battle in the world of market forces. Of this world, a free press is an indispensable part, while a libertine press may be a lethal one.

The ideal of the future Monarchy is served in different ways by different members of the Royal Family. To start with, four examples will be looked at here, all four belonging to the first category of the "inside view" mentioned above.

The Queen herself is consciously dedicated to the strengthening and preservation of the British Monarchy. Her Coronation oath may have suggested a wider patriotism. However, it is through a stable royal system that she sees herself as serving the country and the Commonwealth. As James Callaghan said when describing his prime ministerial audiences with Elizabeth II: "I think she is absolutely right to be on the alert. I think the prestige of the Monarchy could deteriorate if she didn't work so hard at it. . . . She really knows about preserving the Monarchy. . . . When to step into the limelight, when to step out. She really is professional in her approach."

It seems likely that her professionalism will urge her to endure more rather than less of the limelight in the present troubles. After all, no one has yet breached the family's surest defence, "She's never put a foot wrong," whereas the patter of royal feet going astray has become familiar elsewhere.

The Duke of Edinburgh's "inner view" has always been the same and has never faltered. He once explained that some people mistakenly believed the Monarchy existed for the good of the Royal Family. On the contrary, it existed for the good of the people, he said. If the people ever began to feel the opposite, it would be time to bow out. "And for God's sake let us go without a row." In the convincing words of Martin Charteris, "Prince Philip has done a wonderful job for the Monarchy," specifically by being the first to bring it into the twentieth century. But in the Prince's own words, the whole of this job is for the people — from the Awards and World Wild Life Fund to the royal participation in Europe and the Commonwealth. It was on behalf of the British people that he attended the Bonn service in October 1992. There, as part of a special act of reconciliation, he read aloud in German — the only one of his family who was capable of that particular contribution.

Prince Charles is another of the "inside family" who sees the future of the Monarchy as his guiding star. In sketching his immensely detailed and complicated map of projects all over the United Kingdom and beyond — lively and informal as a patchwork but also possessing the commitment of a crusade — he sums it all up in a few words: "My aim is to be useful to the Monarchy."

From a quite different royal quarter there comes a curious example of how the Royal Family sees itself at the present time. This example illustrates the tenacious hold that monarchy in the abstract exerts over its supporters. Marina Mowatt is reported to have described the totally committed feelings of her mother, Princess Alexandra: "My mother puts the Royal Family first, even before her own family." Though it is unnecessary to accept this as a literal account of her mother's feelings, there is evidently something in it — perhaps no less and no more than a soldier would feel who put duty to his country first, or a police officer who must risk his life in the last resort despite wife and children.

The second aspect of the Monarchy on which there is widespread "inside" agreement concerns morality: setting an example. It is remarkable for how relatively short a time the British Royal Family has championed this idea, yet how fervently it is advocated today. George IV in the early nineteenth century would have been astonished to hear that he was "the first gentleman" in Europe, in the sense of being the morally best: most powerful, wealthy, handsome, elegant, cultivated, desirable — yes; but moral — no. Morality belonged, if anywhere, to his private life. Walter Bagehot, writing some fifty years later would still find himself closer in this respect to George IV than to the King's niece, Queen Victoria. It was impossible, thought Bagehot, for any human family, royal or not, to be "head of our morality". And if anyone pointed to Queen Victoria and said that she was just that, Bagehot would have called her the exception that proved the rule. Nevertheless, Victoria herself had already seized hold of the idea quite early in her reign and was not to let it go. She wrote in her *Journal* in 1844: "They say no Sovereign was ever more loved than I am (I am bold to say), & *this* because of our domestic home. The good example it presents." Twenty-two years later, a lonely widow, she was still saying the same thing: her popularity depended as always on "hard work and domestic purity".

The good life for a royal person became, by the next century, inextricably entwined with family life. At the time of her Silver Jubilee in 1977, Elizabeth II came out strongly for family life. Marriage, she said, "must be held firm in the web of family relationships — between parents and children, grandparents and grandchildren, cousins, aunts and uncles". This was a tall order and must be remembered when we come to consider suggestions for cutting the Royal Family down to size.

There is no reason to think that the Queen does not still believe in setting an example of family life twenty years later. Though whether today she could again make the speech she once, as a Princess, addressed to young wives and mothers is doubtful. The date was 1949 and she was drawing attention in her rather high girlish voice to the ravages of divorce: "We live in an age of growing self-indulgence, of hardening materialism, and of falling moral standards. Some of the very principles on which the family is founded are in danger." She went on to name "divorce and separation" as being responsible for "some of the darkest evils in our society". Yet fear of being called "priggish" or "intolerant" prevented us from condemning what we knew to be wrong. Today both her hopes and her voice would be lower. However, it would be for reasons other than fear of being called priggish that she might speak differently in 1993 — perhaps tact and forgiveness, as mentioned in her Christmas message of 1984, delivered after the birth of Prince Harry: "Children teach us forgiveness, without which families are divided."

How does the idea of "setting an example" appeal to those on a different part of the royal spectrum? HRH Prince Michael of Kent is, apart from the Prince of Wales, the only Royal Highness who did not, in 1992, receive a penny from the Civil List. As the younger son of a royal duke — George, Duke of Kent — he had no entitlement to expenses from the public purse. If he took on a job in the public interest, his expenses were a matter — or not — for the cause he served. Otherwise he earned his living like the rest of his contemporaries. In this entirely honourable but anomalous situation he was supported by his wife, Princess Marie-Christine, his son, Lord Frederick Windsor, and his daughter, Lady Gabriella. Being thrown on the world, so to speak, seems to have injected him and his family with valuable adrenalin, his wife being an author and Freddie winning a scholarship to Eton. One might think that "setting a good example" would have ceased to interest the Kents, along with the Civil List. On the contrary, Prince Michael has emphatic views on the question:

Yes, *all* members of the Royal Family, near and far, must set the example of doing their duty, or the thing won't work. Children must be specially brought up to understand this. People are looking at you to give some kind of lead, and there is a terrible danger you fall into if you are seen to have the trappings and not pull your weight. As for outsiders and the problem of making them understand, it can be explained to each new generation, and those on the edges don't have the spotlight to the same extent.*

Handsome, bearded Prince Michael is just what modern royalty should be, says Ingrid Seward, editor of *Majesty*. "He is a true Prince. What he cannot change he accepts, and what he cannot accept he changes."

As one of the younger generation, the Prince of Wales has

*Queen Victoria used to invite each of her future daughters-in-law to pay her "a little visit" at Windsor before marriage. The ostensible reason was so that she could get to know them. I suspect that the real reason was for them to get to know *her*: the Queen, and the ways and traditions of the family.

no difficulty about fitting the idea of "setting an example" into his concept of duty. But like most of the under-fifties, Prince Charles thinks in terms of positive social action rather than of "good behaviour" in Queen Victoria's sense. In an interview as long ago as 1979, Charles saw his duty as "leadership". And what kind of leadership could he give? "I think it is trying to set an example," he explained, using the word "example" in the sense above.

From this was to grow, during the next decade, a multitude of impulses and initiatives that many businessmen, landlords, farmers and builders have been more than eager to follow. Recently, for instance, the Prince discovered a new, neglected area where his own enthusiasm could set an "example": this time to the teachers of English literature in Britain's universities and schools. A summer school inspired by him is on the way, perhaps in Oxford or Stratford, where schoolrooms and lecture halls will echo once again to the voice and name of Shakespeare.

A third "inside view" that is widely and sometimes bitterly held relates, of course, to the press. It is no exaggeration to say that the Royal Family see themselves as engaged in what is at best perpetual duels and at worst confused skirmishes that beset them from all sides and all angles at the same time. This is such a basic subject that it requires space and discussion in a later chapter. It is enough to point out for the present what a distance the Royal Family have travelled since the last century. As far as Queen Victoria was concerned, she regarded the editor of *The Times* as an unofficial channel for her own influence. In her extreme old age, for example, when Britain was fighting the Boers in South Africa, she thought nothing of getting on to the Duke of Devonshire and ordering him to keep *The Times* "straight" on the war. It never crossed her mind that "the Thunderer" might have another voice. There were no tabloids, as her descendants would know them, to be feared and hated. Even ten years after her death, when her grandson Georgie, Prince of Wales, had to bring an action for criminal libel against the journalist Edward Frederick Mylius — "the heir to the throne was a bigamist" — no time was lost in getting the accused a sharp rather than a short sentence: one year inside. Admittedly it was the kind of case that the Palace would almost welcome today: concentrated and clear-cut. The Myliuses of the present age are too clever to tell palpable lies and yet they are always on the job. Prince Philip has said that his married life began (in 1947) "as a private event with a public dimension". Forty-five years later his eldest son may feel that *his* married life is a public event with a private dimension. To adapt an epigram that was first spoken of the Monarchy itself in the eighteenth century, the Royal Family might well agree that the power of the press has increased, is increasing and ought to be diminished.

That Elizabeth II hopes to bring about some sort of diminution seems more than likely. Consider the following newsflash which appeared in *The Times* on 25 October 1992:

Queen seeks curb on press invasion of royal privacy. Buckingham Palace confirmed last night that Charles Anson, the Queen's press secretary, has given oral evidence to Sir David Calcutt QC, who is conducting a review of the press on behalf of the Government. Calcutt is due to report to the Government in January 1993.

Passages like the above seemed to appear more and more often in the papers, always listing, at that date, the same private incidents as examples of press licence: the Princess of Wales's telephone calls to a male friend ("Dianagate") and the photographs of the Duchess of York with her financial adviser. It would be strange if no efforts were being made behind the scenes to work out with the Government ways of putting tighter curbs on a press that would nevertheless still be called "free". The point is, can it be done? For the Royal Family have left us in no doubt that they do, despite everything, believe in a free press. In his usual astringent and lucid way, the Duke of Edinburgh has once and for all put his seal to civilisation's precious guarantee. "No society that values its liberty", he said, "can do without the freedom to discuss and indeed to gossip about . . . institutions and events" — bearing in mind that the Monarchy is an institution particularly famous for events that are gossip-worthy.

So far we have looked at three attitudes taken to the Monarchy by the Royal Family on which they virtually all agree: the Monarchy's transcendent value, its duty to set an example, and its problem with the press. Fourth and last comes its religious overtone. Sir Robert Fellowes put a pertinent question about these issues: "How do you distinguish between the Monarchy and the Royal Family?" (How an earlier generation of the Royal Household tackled this question has already been looked at in the first chapter.) That will need discussing when we finally reach the point-blank question of the Monarchy's survival.

Meanwhile, in analysing the spiritual dimension of the Monarchy, it is enough to point out at the moment two conflicting issues. In principle, the Monarchy stands above and beyond the royal individuals who happen to represent it at any given time. In practice, the misfortunes of royal individuals could affect the whole fabric. For example, if the Prince of Wales were to be divorced, could he become head of a church whose canon law forbade divorce? There are several possible answers: the Church could be disestablished — made independent of the State and so of the Monarchy; or the Church's law on divorce could be changed; or some accommodation could be found within the Church as it is. Whatever solution were to be adopted, we could be sure of one thing: divorce would not rule out King Charles III — provided the country wanted him.

Apart from these considerations, we can recall a characteristically sensitive comment by Queen Elizabeth the Queen Mother. Speaking of her Coronation she said: "You never feel the same again." A similar conviction of something irrevocable having taken place at her own Coronation clearly possesses Queen Elizabeth II. She said, talking of possible separatist tendencies in her realms, "I can never forget that I was crowned Queen of the United Kingdom of Great Britain and Northern Ireland." At their Coronations, mother and daughter both felt charged in some way, once and for all; Elizabeth II perhaps even more radically, since she had been anointed Queen Regnant rather than Queen Consort. At the same time, each felt equally emboldened to do everything within her power to maintain the gift of royal privilege and obligation bestowed on her by the holy oil: the Queen Mother gallantly opening new wings at the age of ninety-two, just when she might be forgiven for folding her own; Elizabeth II travelling all over the United Kingdom and the world, risking bad eggs in Bonn rather than allow any external pressure or internal weakness to harm the future of the Monarchy. The writer Robert Graves once made a celebrated remark after an audience with the young Elizabeth II: "The holy oil has taken for that girl! It worked for her all right!" We may be sure that in the present troubles she will do everything to make the holy oil work for her again.

The Queen's children will not have exactly the same "inside view" of the Monarchy as their mother. It is natural that the two younger Princes, Andrew and Edward, and their sister, Princess Anne, should minimise as far as possible their royal birth when directing a dramatic performance or jumping for England — not to mention bringing food to the starving. Both the Duke of York and the Princess Royal have given the impression that they could do without the royal *frisson*, spiritual or temporal, except in the last resort. Andrew has been reported as saying, "I become bored with myself and like taking on other roles and characters," while his sister once exclaimed, "I didn't ask to be born a Princess." Especially if it meant being kidnapped in The Mall — or nearly so — or, in Edward's case, being picked out for special anti-royal kicks during a game of rugger at college. Perhaps the most striking case of a royal child regarding the Monarchy with deep suspicion, almost as a *damna hereditas*, occurred in the childhood of Princess Margaret. It was 10 December 1936. Princess Elizabeth, her sister, had just heard from a footman at their home, Clarence House, that Uncle David had abdicated and Papa was King. She dashed upstairs to tell Margaret Rose.

"Does that mean you will have to be the next Queen?" asked the precocious six year old.

"Yes, some day."

"Poor you."

We have seen that among the Queen's three younger children there is a natural instinct to bypass to some extent their connection with the Monarchy and to find their individual selves. With the eldest son things are quite different. True, there exist the signs of a modest personality shrinking into deliberate colourlessness after periods of over-exposure. On the whole, however, his focus is unerringly fixed upon his relation to the Monarchy. Prince Charles may not have asked to be born a Prince, but since he *is* Prince of Wales, he intends to leave his mark on the Monarchy — now and in the future — rather than the Monarchy leaving its mark on him. To be sure, that unassuming image is never entirely out of sight. "I am so bored with my face," he said at the age of twenty-one, "can't we have someone else?" It is the same endearing feeling that prompted him as a small Cheam schoolboy to kneel in church at matins and think: "I wish that they prayed for the other boys too."

Then there are the rare and happy adult moments when he can become an "Honorary Ordinary Bloke". This is generally through contact with his tenant farmers in the Duchy of Cornwall, or through sport. In that sense he is not so very different from any country gentleman who might mingle with the locals at the Farmers' Club or on the village cricket field. The Prince's use of the term "ordinary bloke" links him with his father, who also likes both the type and the words. In Suzy Menkes's striking study of the Royal Family as country people at heart* we are presented with

Queen and Country (1992).

83

Prince Philip's favourite "ordinary bloke", one "Geordie" Bowman, a scrapmerchant turned driver. "Backgrounds don't come into our sport," he says. Having produced his team of horses at the Sandringham trials, he has taught them to bend their huge hairy knees to the Queen.

But in spite of all the charming ordinary blokes with whom the Prince of Wales can assimilate in Cornwall or Gloucestershire, the royal factor remains paramount. After describing his background and upbringing to interviewers Charles would add: "So it makes one different, and it makes one feel different."

How does this feeling of difference, this actually *being* different, as the Prince believes, affect his inside view of the Monarchy? In his mid-forties, he no longer uses his very active imagination for writing fairy stories — an Old Man of Lochnagar for his brothers or even a Young Man of Lochnagar for his sons — but to get things done. "I don't want to be a figure-head," he says; "I want to get things done." When the Prince uses that phrase, his audience is apt to think sceptically of King Edward VIII, who, having been genuinely shocked by unemployment in the South Wales coalfields and having demanded action — "Something must be done" — left it for someone else to do. But experience has already taught us that Prince Charles is a man of action rather than a wordsmith. And he sees no source of available energy and action more effective than the Monarchy at work. In past times there were arguments in favour of the Monarchy keeping a low profile. There was always a certain amount of suspicion: was some member of the Royal Family plotting to snatch back an aspect of political power that Parliament had long ago fought and won a civil war to hold in trust for the people? When the future William IV, then Duke of Clarence and Lord High Admiral, put to sea with the grand fleet but without his council's permission, he lost his job.

Today "the rules of the game have changed", as Ferdinand Mount puts it. There will be critics still, no doubt, to disagree with the Prince of Wales's ideas and consequently feel that his position gives him an unfair advantage when it comes to argument. Nevertheless, there are few restrictions on what the Prince can do for the country, even where money is involved. In the last chapter we shall see how the future of the Monarchy depends basically on its guardianship of the constitution, much less on the presence or absence of one particular royal interest, such as collecting paintings, like Charles I and Prince Albert, or raising pedigree cattle, like Elizabeth II. Both those royal occupations have greatly benefited the country, but people take them for granted. The remarkable thing about Prince Charles's activities is their originality. In the last decade, for instance, he has discovered a way in which he can help "to put the Great back into Britain", by means of travels into Europe.

"It's very sad to see a great country no longer," he says, ending on a sigh. "I may be wrong, but I feel we've got a great deal to learn from the Europeans. But we're insular, don't like learning from foreigners. In industry and education we should *learn*, and then adapt to the British way. It is *frustrating* the way things are."

Beware of misinterpreting his word "frustrating". The Prince is by no means frustrated by any intrinsic constraints to his position. He visualises his ideas being accepted, but only after many battles against the sceptics.

Take the foreign Chambers of Commerce [he continues]; here they are very individualistic. We could learn a great deal from them in industrial terms. The German ones have enormous impact on local and business affairs. As a company, you have to by law belong to a Chamber of Commerce. Whereas you get agencies here and other organisations there, but no co-ordination, say, when something is invented. Our methods are *disparate.* Where there are Chambers of Commerce they are relatively ineffective. You should see Japan. . . .

When asked how he came to form all these opinions he replied:

From travel in foreign countries. Half the battle is to learn from things that work. There is need to analyse what are the ingredients of someone else's success. The Germans are particularly good at marketing, for instance, but for some reason we are terribly reluctant to learn from others.

The Prince's mind also plays on education and the potentialities there:

Well, Prince Albert — when he died he was years younger than I am now [Prince Albert was forty-two to Prince Charles's forty-three!] — he tried to introduce Continental ways especially in education and science: as a result he was totally misunderstood.

Take education today. There have been countless Enquiries since the 1950s — nothing has ever been basically changed. In the German and French systems corresponding to A Levels (French Baccalauréat, German Abitur) they don't specialise, they have a much broader education; but not only that, they stay on longer at school, which I also think is important. I could never have decided what I wanted to do at sixteen, unless I was exceptionally gifted.

In Germany they have vocational education alongside academic of equal status. Here engineers and such-like are looked down on. But you only have proper status if you have the qualifications. Nothing is ever perfect, but we could improve our chances in this incredibly difficult situation.

Last year we had a great conference in a tent, in a marquee on the lawn at Highgrove with people from industry and academics to discuss the whole question of *innovation*. We are notoriously bad at making the most of our inventions. Others pick up our ideas. They make money and we lose the whole way along the line.

The Committee set up by this conference recommended institutions and agencies which would exist between the academic world and industry — "Faraday Institutes". Of course they would require considerable funds to set them up. This would be a worthwhile long-term investment in the future. But "they" are terribly terribly reluctant to spend money now, to get something back in five or ten years' time.

It was suggested that the country was highly dissatisfied with itself at the present time, so this might be the moment for the Prince to put the boot in.

But if I do, I shall hear that I am a socialist! Because I talk about things to do with the Community, the public good (which one has to consider in a civilised society), I was accused by someone who came to lunch with us of having "wishy-washy socialist ideas". So I'm suspect!

However if the Prince lands in a different part of Europe from Germany, say Brussels instead of Bonn, he may be accused of having "wishy-washy individualistic ideas":

Of course I entirely understand the wish to unite and get away from European nationalism . . . but there is an obsession with standardising everything — such things as cheese and fruit — by bureaucrats. There is need to stop interference with the nuts and bolts of people's lives. Intolerable! It's not what an integrated Europe should be about. It's interference under the guise of hygiene. In my garden are rare and old-fashioned vegetables but now shops can't sell them — Women's Institute shops can't sell them, because they don't conform to some ludicrous regulation!

So here the Prince of Wales stands, not exactly a future monarch with his head on the block, but at any rate a protesting spirit first at one end and then at the other end of the see-saw between outrageous regulation and short-sighted free for all. It might be thought that this "inside" view, if uncomfortable, could be the right kind of balancing act for a future monarch.

A few years ago it might have been difficult to track down the Queen's personal "inside" view of the Monarchy. Since her more extensive use of television, however, as a medium of communication, the Queen herself seems to have laid some deliberate clues. The film *Elizabeth R* by Antony Jay and Michael Mirzoeff has the largest number in the smallest space. Perhaps the most interesting are grouped around the Queen's work. Top of her list comes the royal relationship with prime ministers.

"I think it is rather nice to feel one's a sort of sponge," she says whimsically. "And everyone can come and tell one things and some things go out the other ear. And some things never come out at all. One just knows about it. And occasionally you are able to put your point of view. Perhaps they hadn't seen it from that angle."

The Queen realises that prime ministers sometimes want to unburden themselves, particularly to a monarch who is impartial (in the sense of doing her best for each and every one of them).

There follows the greatest understatement of all time, yet a statement full of wise self-knowledge. "If you live this sort of life," said the Queen, "which people don't very much, you live very much by tradition and by continuity."

The Queen had admitted earlier that nothing much changes in her life, though holidays at Balmoral produced one thing that was quite unique: "To hibernate is rather nice when one leads such a very movable life — to be able to sleep in the same bed for six weeks is a nice change." This in itself is a surprise. How strange that Britain's age-old Monarchy should strike today's august representative as being above all things mobile. But she is right, if we think of the royal train, Queen's flight, cars, royal yacht, Bonn, Dresden, Paris, Normandy, Canada, Australia, the United States.

Prime ministers are not the only people that the Queen has in her mind when she considers the work of the Crown. The film of *Elizabeth R* shows her taking an altogether more serious interest in personal communication than might have been supposed. Walkabouts, for example. In the old days, walkabouts seemed fairly haphazard, spontaneous affairs that were aptly described by the new folkword. To go walkabout in these days is something to be planned meticulously by the Queen and her staff for a most specific purpose: "A lot of people don't come to London very often," she says, "and we travel to them instead." (By "we" she means herself and Prince Philip, not a royal "we".) Sometimes they will have to go flyabout or driveabout — "Thus do go about, about", like the witches in *Macbeth*, except that they are guardian spirits.

One of the 200 to 300 letters a day that come to the Queen may ask for special help. The Queen will do the necessary readabout and, if she is able to respond, there will be no passing of the buck. A feeling of intense satisfaction seemed to fill the Queen as she spoke those simple words in her film: "There are occasions when I can help. The buck stops here."

The Queen thinks of all these people as her special responsibility. They make the job worthwhile. How do they think of her?

CHAPTER
FIVE

How Others View the Royal Family

[Bishop] Michael Mann is one of those (Bishop Woods is another) who would welcome a small council of elder statesmen and women, independent of the Palace, who would be invited to offer advice to the Queen which she could either accept or reject. . . .

Two former Deans of Windsor talking to Douglas Keay in his Elizabeth II, *updated 1992*

A point has been reached when people might be forgiven for seeing the Monarchy not only through a glass darkly but also through a cross-eyed press, crookedly. Take the week of Armistice Day 1992. Photographers managed to suggest anything but the drama we were actually celebrating at the Cenotaph: the sacrifices of two World Wars, the Falklands War, the Gulf War and Europe still tossing in a Balkan fever. Instead, there was the vision of Princess Diana throwing one of her sweet sidelong glances at the Princess Royal, who apparently *scowled* back. What did it all mean?

Perhaps it was a good thing that the Prince of Wales was not laying his poppy wreath on the Cenotaph but on a monument in Hong Kong. At least the "royal watchers" were prevented from measuring the distance between him and his wife.

Most people depend partly on the press for their view of the Monarchy, and by autumn 1992 that view was more than contradictory — it was chaotic. Those people who rely on television for their royal image get less speculation and invention but also less day-by-day detail. A television programme in September, for instance, presented the Prince and Princess of Wales as two young people with a heavy load of work to carry out while at the same time having to live up to a tremendous superstructure of myth. Fair enough. True, someone offered a picture of Prince Charles as "the world's most difficult husband", but there was always someone else to hail him as an idealist, a popular father to his school-age children (they rush to him when he arrives home), a good man. It is noticeable that those who rely on television have more confidence in the Monarchy's future than those who read the tabloids. Here, however, lurks a paradox. It is the tabloids who would suffer most if anything happened to the Monarchy.

Imagine a normal newspaper reader trying to work out the future of the British Crown from its showing during the summer and autumn of 1992. In the (June) *Daily Mirror*, we were told that "tragic patients weep with joy at Princess's visit" to a hospice for the dying. "This is why we need her." In the (July) *Sunday Telegraph* she is seen by Mary Kenny in "competition" with her husband for Mother Teresa of Calcutta's endorsement and "going into a teenage sulk if her husband gets to send the flowers to M.T. first". "Good Lord," continues the redoubtable Kenny, "why couldn't the Royals have found Charles some sensible young woman out of Cheltenham Ladies' College with a bit of moral fibre to her? Someone who understood the very tough job entailed in being a Princess of Wales? Where are all those memsahibs who stomped across the North-West Frontier without complaining? They must have distributed their genes somewhere."

If we look at the script for the dramas around Armistice week there is farce and fraudulence.

4 November: A South Korean lady in the crowd welcoming the Waleses to Seoul thinks she is greeting "Diana and *Philip*". It makes her so happy. While the Prince of Wales is delivering his official speech, we are told, the Princess is busy "smirking" at the listening journalists. On the same day as these oriental happenings, the *Sun* is preparing another "royal blockbuster": Andrew Morton's paperback with its serialised new chapter "A Princess Alone". Diana is photographed as a "forlorn and lonely figure in front of the beautiful Taj Mahal", which, the *Sun* kindly explains, is "India's temple of love". In fact, the Taj Mahal is a royal mausoleum.

We are told that Morton again has "well-placed sources" (though unnamed this time) and we are promised "the full story behind the explosive letter written by Prince Philip to Di and her furious reply".

5 November: The first of the "well-placed sources" is revealed by the *Evening Standard* to have placed himself well out of reach. From Adelaide, Australia, James Gilbey tells the Londoner's Diary that he has not helped Morton at all with the new chapter. Gilbey's friends say: "He's getting fed up with Morton altogether. He just wants to get away from it all." On the same auspicious date (Guy Fawkes' Day), a tabloid accuses the Queen of having been "callous" to Diana while Prince Philip has sent a "poison pen letter" to her; she herself is lined up to announce tomorrow: "This family will destroy me."

6 November: Tomorrow came, and Diana said it in full in the *Mirror*: "If I don't escape from this family soon, they will totally destroy me." However, on the very next day, the 7th, after the Princess of Wales was planning "escape-or-else . . .", according to the tabloids, she was issuing on her own behalf an unexpectedly different statement to the press:

> The Princess of Wales would like to single out from the recent wave of misleading reports about the royal family assertions in some newspapers this week directed specifically against the Queen and the Duke of Edinburgh. The suggestion that they have been anything other than sympathetic and supportive is untrue and particularly hurtful.

It was a statement that the Prince of Wales "warmly endorsed". If this was one week in the life of the Royal Family, what have the months and years in store?

Fortunately, the people's judgment of the Monarchy is widely based. The unhappy events of 1992 will certainly affect their view. But they have all sorts of tentacles — personal memories, folk memories — stretching into the recent or distant past, all of which will contribute to their final assessment of what it means to live in a kingdom rather than a republic. Some of those who were gazing at the Cenotaph on Remembrance Sunday may even have held in a corner of memory the fact that King Charles I died close by. The present Royal Family shares the same blood as Charles not as Cromwell. We have tried a republic, after a civil war, and it did not work. Why try it again?

Lined up at the Cenotaph was a figure even more nostalgic than the ghost of Charles I, a figure that has held the Royal Family together for more years than most people can remember and still does so. "Without her", writes Philip Howard, "it might have lost its job." It seems strange in a way that someone as diaphanous as the Queen Mother — all chiffon and sparkles — should turn out to be a pillar of strength to the Monarchy. Even stranger, perhaps, that she should have brought back into the family the longevity that seemed to have gone out with Queen Victoria's children (Louise and Arthur both lived to be over ninety-one). But today the Queen Mother is still the apotheosis of royalty in the modern world. It is to her that her grandson, Prince Charles, turns for "fun, laughter, warmth, infinite security", and he speaks of people falling under her spell, and of the "impact she has made on her century". The Queen, her daughter, when congratulated on doing something well, is apt to comment, "Yes, but Mummy would have done it better."

As with most remarkable characters, people see in her traits that are complementary if not contradictory. She is so natural and unaffected that no one forgets she was born a commoner — "one of us" — yet, at the same time, she is a grand performer. She puts on the best kind of act. Before a speech she tells people she is terribly nervous, but no one would believe it from the way she speaks directly to her audience; after the speech she and her audience are one. She is gentle and soothing, though with steely resolve. It was she who smoothed away her husband's "gnashes" (rages) with jokes and smiles; it was she who got the Royal Family through the war and post-war era. If Prince Philip was the one who carried them into the twentieth century, she was the one who made the twentieth century feel that they had got a rare and worthwhile thing in the Monarchy.

The Queen Mother is also fortunate in having a style of her own and a way of speaking that people can recognise and remember. "One never knows what to wear," she says, with a wry tribute to the English weather, but whatever she chooses it looks effervescent. A favourite parlour game used to consist of asking, "What runs in their veins?", the possibilities ranging from cyanide to honey. In Queen Elizabeth's veins quite obviously flows vintage champagne. The steel in her make-up caused her to declare for a personal Resistance if the Nazis arrived, whatever might have happened to her fellow crowned heads. "I shall not go down with the others," she said, flourishing her revolver. The poor saw that she cared. When a stick of bombs was dropped over the Palace by the Luftwaffe, she said, "I'm glad we've been bombed. Now I can look the East End in the face." A few people have contradicted her, arguing that no one who lives in a palace can have the same experiences as East Enders. Not so. Though they cannot over small things perhaps, they can over the big ones; being crushed by a palace is no pleasanter than being buried by a hovel.

True, it is easier for a monarchy to flourish in time of war than in periods of deflation and unease, when no heroic demands are made of people or leaders. Provided the war is not going disastrously — when a revolution and the end of a royal house may result — people will cling to authority and respond to calls for self-sacrifice, particularly if they see that the family that makes the calls is also making some of the sacrifices. The death of Prince George of Kent in the war created a special empathy between the Royal Family and the people.

It was easier still for the Monarchy to succeed in the days of Edward VII. Just win the Derby and all was happy and glorious. Today the problems for the Crown are multiplying. We are told by some political leaders that we are a second-rate country, yet instead of being urged to make our way back to the top rank, people are only required to put up patiently with worklessness. Parliament's golden leaders seem to be missing. Its reputation, if not in shreds, is a thing of patches. This would be the time for people to see the same kind of decline in the Monarchy. But do they?

No one denies that the Royal Family work much harder today than ever before. Michael Adeane, the Queen's private secretary, first pointed it out in 1971 and the process has gone on ever since. Who would expect their own granny to go on fulfilling engagements, public or otherwise, at the age of ninety-two? When Princess Louise was seventy-six, her brother Prince Arthur advised her not to do any functions in the winter that meant going outdoors — "you really must chuck such functions" — *he* couldn't face them and she was older than him, and a woman! Yet at ninety-two the Queen Mother was coming out in the cold and darkness of a November evening to open the new extension of the London Library, of which she is patron — chatting to members about the pleasures of reading or deploring the very recent burning of Windsor Castle.

The public's appreciation of their seventy-year-old Prince Consort is sophisticated and assured. People tried at first to saddle Prince Philip with a replica image of Prince Albert, on the strength of his having modernised Buckingham Palace for Elizabeth II in much the same way as Albert had done it for Victoria. Prince Philip also shared Prince Albert's intellectual curiosity, that led them both to find inspiration in science and philosophical thought. Prince Philip, however, was able to carry out his modernisation more effectively — poor Albert failed to cure the toxic drains at Windsor which were eventually to destroy him — while the Duke of Edinburgh's "questioning spirit" (learnt from Kurt Hahn, the German educationist) inspired him to spread his work for the environment world-wide instead of just in Britain.

The public has discovered faults — where would it not? — in a temperament that cannot suffer fools equably, is impatient and occasionally flies storm signals, though only for a passing moment. These are the faults of vitality, keenness, perfectionism, not of self-satisfaction or self-indulgence. He has been called a bully. To be a green mystic — as he is — and also at the same time a bully is too unlikely to be readily accepted. And, indeed, reports on the private man show him to be sensitive and kindly. He visits the widow and the fatherless. When there is a state function under way, he will go down to the kitchens, look inside the saucepans and generally show "morale-boosting" interest. It was in his day that all staff were able to take their families and pets with them to Balmoral for the whole royal holiday. In the days of Queen Victoria even her enormously respected private secretary, Sir Henry Ponsonby, was not allowed to take his wife; she had to be left behind at Windsor.

Apart from the alleged bullying, I suspect that he is often a tease. At a royal garden party I once wore a gaudy hat strewn with far too many white feathers. He looked at it doubtfully. "Where did it come from?" "Paris," I said. "Sent in a package all ready to be put together at this end." "Ah, I see. A do-it-yourself hat." Prince Philip can also make jokes against himself. To loud applause he began his speech at Princess Anne's (first) wedding breakfast with the words, "Unaccustomed as I am — to speaking at breakfast. . . ."

More seriously, he has been seen as bullying his eldest son. There are several points to be made in answer to this. Prince Charles has no uncles to do what many uncles do, speak to their nephews "like a father". While Lord Mountbatten was alive he could and did perform that function — and greatly did he enjoy it. "It's not luck at all," he said, that the country had such a splendid heir to the throne; "it's a bloody miracle." Great-uncle Dickie's bloody murder, however, made it harder to benefit fully from the bloody miracle. The date of the assassination was 1979, two years before Prince Charles's marriage. As one close to the Royal Family has said, "Philip speaks out frankly and openly to his son and heir and he is the only man who can. To do so is his manifest duty."

It is, of course, somewhat dangerous to use an imperative like "manifest" when it is a question of the Duke of Edinburgh. One writer had the ill-luck to entitle a book on Lord Mountbatten of Burma *Manifest Destiny*, to which the Duke riposted, "Manifest Bunkum".

The Prince of Wales may well be in awe of his father, but he is also deeply attached to him and full of admiration. When he was shown a letter written by the Iron Duke on the eve of the battle of Waterloo, he was immediately reminded of his father: the same outward unflappability with underneath a reservoir of deep emotions.

Visitors to the Duke of Edinburgh's office in Buckingham Palace have reported that there are no photographs of Prince Charles, only of Princess Anne — the inference being that the Duke could not stick his son. But it is possible to think of many a British father who would never linger fondly over the photograph of a son, however much that son was beloved.

Far more pernicious than these trivialities is the paragraph about the relations of Prince Philip and Prince Charles in the egregious Morton's *Diana: Her True Story*. The Princess of Wales is reported as calling their relationship "tricky, very tricky"; Morton, in fact, implies that the older man is contemptibly jealous. "It rankles with Prince Philip", for instance, "that he started the discussion about the environment but it was Prince Charles who got the audience."

Prince Charles is powerfully influenced by his father and has developed some of the same ideas, often adopting the same language. They are both passionately anti-litter, bent on working with instead of against nature, and deeply committed to the deprived. "I do not have a 'job' but aim to start various initiatives," said Prince Philip to his biographer, Tim Heald. Similarly we have seen that Prince Charles speaks of giving an "impetus" to affairs, a word having the same meaning as "initiative" though with a somewhat more explosive overtone. As a matter of fact it was old Baron Stockmar who first introduced the notion of "impetus" or "impulse" into the royal thinking. He told Prince Albert when he first took over the Duchy of Cornwall: "It is for you to give only the impulse, to establish sound principles." The truth is that in old age and middle age respectively, the pair are bound together in mutual understanding and empathy.

But those who would not dream of bringing the word "bully" into this two-way association will nevertheless sometimes see the inner Royal Family as a whole bullying the outer fringes — or any other group that seems to threaten or hamper them. However, most small groups tend to band together in self-protection and it is doubtful whether that kind of behaviour, even if it exists, would be widely noticed or would affect to any real extent the future of the Monarchy.

Princess Anne could stand a good chance of winning the popularity stakes within the Royal Family. She enjoys a special relationship with her father — his only daughter — through character affinities. Her notorious "Naff off!" to intrusive journalists has been forgiven. She has graduated from holding the palm in bad-tempered cussedness to winning top awards for solid achievements, all pursued in a spirit of practical no nonsense. Riding is now for the disabled not for the winning-post. It is quite impossible to imagine her sharing the attitude of her two sisters-in-law to, say, the Saturday morning shopping spree. And the fact that she was once cast as the "baddie" in the royal soap opera is no obstacle to her being very good news now; rather the opposite. The public likes a recognisable cast with traditional goodies and baddies, but it is volatile. It likes a change. At the moment there is an abandoned character around called "Fergie", who plays her part well, and two other possible actors who pop in and out of the entrances marked "Rain" and "Sun", like two little figures in a Swiss barometer. Sometimes it is the Princess of Wales who is on the "fine" side of the popular weather-glass, while the media stormclouds burst over the unlucky Prince. At other times the Princess is the one who gets a drenching.

Meanwhile, Princess Anne is one of the royals who will outlast all challengers. She once became the Third Most Popular Woman in the World after the Queen and Mrs Golda Meir — not a pinnacle perhaps, but meritorious. She got there not through evanescent gifts like fashion sense, but because of courage, endurance and determination. No one else would have dared to let slip the two revealing remarks she made about her lifework — the Save the Children Fund. She questioned, by implication at least, the motives of public figures who take on enormously prominent jobs. Is it partly for self-advertisement or purely for the cause? "I hope I have accepted for the right reasons," she said. More astonishing still, she had the nerve to admit that she was not an over-the-top adorer of children; she just recognised their rights and intended to see that they got them. And so, as a result of exceptional honesty and forthrightness, she could, in due course, do no wrong. She had been "de-naffed" and dubbed "the latterday Florence Nightingale". If the Prince of Wales were to be located abroad performing some public duty on his son William's birthday, he would never hear the last of it. On her son Peter's fourth birthday Princess Anne was in the Himalayas. So what?

Even her divorce has been forgiven and her second marriage blessed by the public. To be sure, there was some discussion as to whether the daughter of the head of the Church of England should remarry in church, but the quiet wedding in a Scottish church seemed to be generally accepted.

The path of writing royal biographies while the subject is still alive, and of making predictions, is full of potholes and is well illustrated by the fate of the writer Paul James. Hitherto informative and reliable, James's biography, *Anne: The Working Princess* (1987), ran into trouble when it reached the future of her first marriage. "Her family is now complete with a boy and a girl," wrote James; "her marriage, despite the rumours, is solid in its foundations." Five years later she was divorced. James had also risked saying that when the allegedly alienated Mark and Anne had visited Dubai and Abu Dhabi together, it had given "a welcome slap in the face to those speculating about their relationship". Alas, those who received the slap in the face would not have hesitated to turn the other cheek, for there was to be no second slap — except perhaps in the writer's face.

A well-known journalist and writer, Penny Junor, faced the same kind of trouble. She too had estimated as solid the partnership of the Prince and Princess of Wales. In *Charles and Diana* (1992), she wrote: "They have settled down, sorted out their personal problems, adjusted their lives to accommodate each other, found a way to cope with the pressure and emerged with a very strong successful partnership." Penny Junor had not reckoned with the publicity arising from subsequent events and its effect.

What is the lesson to be learnt by writers working in this treacherous zone? Some people think that the Monarchy itself is to blame, because of its tradition of remaining silent when it can see well-intentioned biographers barking up the wrong tree. The royal staff, say their critics, should have permission to give at least a glimpse of the truth. On the other hand, those who are thus expected to give accurate signals at a given moment may not even know themselves what the future is likely to reveal. Prince Philip ironically said to a couple in the crowd on his Silver Wedding walkabout: "How long have you been married? Eleven years? The first twelve years are the worst. After that it's all downhill!" The Waleses had been married for eleven years by 1992, but there was to be no twelfth year to herald a smoother stage. Marriages that go downhill in the bad sense are seldom likely to take two sharply separate routes at a certain clear-cut milestone. Royal spouses in particular, in whose lives so much happens under the glare of publicity (a dazzle that may confuse and render half blind the performers as well as the viewers), can seldom have the chance to see steadily what is going to happen next. In any case, they have probably taken no steps to encourage would-be biographers. It is not their business, surely, to point out the pitfalls. Of course, they should not give deliberately misleading answers, but they are under no obligation to tell all — even on the rare occasions when they themselves know all.

The moral seems to be that neutrality or even scepticism on the part of writers is a safer attitude than optimism, however well-meaning. Of all the royal biographers who have plunged about in these waters during the past decade, Anthony Holden turns out to be one of the least deluded because the least hopeful. Yet even *his* cynical paragraphs can appear now and then to err on the side of confidence. The presence of the Duchess of York, for instance, he saw as "a sheet-anchor" in the lives of Princess Diana and Prince Andrew — an anchor that in fact was to drag badly. Though

Holden's knowledge was as great as Morton's (as appears from reading Holden's book with hindsight), he too could not have reckoned with the effects of *Diana: Her True Story*. Philip Ziegler has called it "Crawfie with strychnine".*

Despite the battering by the media of the Prince of Wales's personal life, there are no real signs that the pollsters' regular report — "The Prince of Wales is doing a good job" — has lost its validity. In other words, he is regarded by most Britons as the right kind of man for the country's future king. That makes him appear conventional and orthodox — and so he is in many ways. His friends are British upper class, from the services and the killing fields. His accent is British upper class. But in each of these cases there is a pronounced paradox attached. The Prince is not so uncomplicated as this makes him sound, and his expensive education was full of contradictions.

First, being sent to Gordonstoun, the British public school which Prince Charles and his two brothers attended *because their father went there*, could not be more "trad". On the other hand, the school was founded by an ultra-modern German pioneer educationist, Kurt Hahn, rather than by, say, King Henry VI, royal pioneer of Eton. It would have been far more "trad" for Charles and his brothers to be Old Etonians. Instead, the heir to the throne was brought up with ideas of toughness and self-testing that might have been familiar to the Black Prince or Prince Hal, but not much since. A modern royal family that could educate its sons in this relentless, uncompromising way could not fail to

*Marion (Crawfie) Crawford, author of *The Little Princesses* (1950), the story of Princess Elizabeth and Princess Margaret, whose governess she was.

appeal to a large section of the British public who might have criticised Eton's airs and graces. However, it also provoked some criticism.

Nor did the paradox attached to the Prince's education stop short at the unorthodoxy of his public school. Charles's schooldays were often pretty miserable; at the same time he strongly approved of what had been pumped into him. He had been forced to cultivate "order and tidiness". You cannot be truly traditional in your feelings — as the Prince is — without a strong sense of order. Reformers, on the contrary, are not generally addicted to order and tidiness, since they cannot know for sure what the new order is going to be. Prince Charles has managed to square his circle by reforming passionately in a traditional direction. Those who approve of him — and they are many — were taught by him to see things like farming and housing through his eyes.

Second, his friends share his own devotion to huntin', fishin', shootin' and farmin', even though "organic farmin'" seems at first sight to be something of a contradiction. It is relatively easy to follow the Prince's arguments in favour of nature and against pesticides and chemical fertilisers. But the arguments of those organic believers who also go hunting and shooting, because wildlife must be culled to remain healthy, seem to assume that this aspect of the equation cannot be left to nature. Why is not Mother Nature herself able to keep the balance between culling and increase? Why does she need bang bang but not spray spray? The public have a healthy instinct that this paradox of "organic blood sports" keeps their Prince normal. If you add his polo to the big four of hunting, fishing, shooting and farming, you can see at once that the future King is in no sense (to quote his own words) someone "robed and shaved, sandalled, with a faraway look in my eyes", in search of a guru.

Polo, besides being an expensive sport redolent of the Raj and what the Raj used to stand for — adventure, fitness, leadership, paternalism — provides the Prince with the ultimate answer to self-testing. If not as dangerous as Prince Andrew's flying exploits in the Falklands, for which his elder brother felt a not ignoble envy, polo has its hair-raising moments. The Prince of Wales's daring at polo (resulting in a fractured arm) convinced *him*, the most important person to require convincing, that he was a man not just a prince. His queueing up in Casualty at the Nottingham hospital for emergency treatment convinced his public that their man was good.

Incidentally, the Royal Family's addiction to horses cannot be exaggerated and, as Prince Charles once said, "I have never known a family so addicted to tea," meaning the five o'clock feast, not just the cuppa. Teatime rounds off a day in the country devoted to walking, jogging or any exhausting outdoor sport, particularly riding. It was the Queen and Queen Mother who excitedly plotted together the secret adventure of owning race-horses; the Duke of Edinburgh moved from polo to carriage-driving; Princess Anne was an eventer of top world performance. There is no doubt that, with the public, the Royal Family's love of horses helps to give them a human face — if not an equine one. Princess Anne once said that people expected her to swish her tail and take her coffee-sugar from the palm of the hand. Horses are the bridge between the family's majesty and their humanity. There is a story of Lord Randolph Churchill making a speech last century in which he described the Monarchy and the people as having three things in common: love of horses, hatred of the middle classes and love of immorality. Lord Randolph's political agent hastily changed the third item into "love of morality". What a pity the first item — horses — did not make a bridge between Prince Charles and Princess Diana.

Third and last, the Prince of Wales's upper-class accent. Here again, there is an interesting overtone, as personal as it is attractive and unexpected, to the familiar voice: what Holden called, "a curious note of apology for being who he is". The anxious lines that tend to gather on the forehead and round the mouth tell the same story. Does he think there may be a frog inside the Prince?

At any rate he will always remember the debt he owes to his country for his privileges. That is why the country will continue to see him as doing a good job. And that is why his characteristic mixture of two opposite qualities — buoyancy and diffidence — will always appeal to fair-minded people. Just as his father's and sister's combination of outspokenness and hard work will always have its admirers.

Nevertheless, there are signs of criticism — one hopes temporary — of the Royal Family that cannot be ignored. Not that this is an unheard-of situation. The Monarchy was questioned in the late 1950s and 1960s, but the significant and perhaps sinister difference today is that the criticism comes mainly from the right. And the right is traditionally supposed to be pro-Crown. Censured in 1957 for an outdated style, the young Queen Elizabeth II abolished Court presentations of débutantes. This and other changes, like walkabouts, exhibitions for the public of royal pictures and intimate

Palace luncheons for ordinary people, were all calculated to please the left. Indeed, one right-wing writer predicted fatal results to the Monarchy from their loss of the "deb" and aristocratic entourage at garden parties and elsewhere. The Throne, it was foreseen, would be left high and dry in an alien world.

However, this was only one reactionary voice in a general chorus of praise. We have to go back to the early days of Queen Victoria and Prince Albert to find disapproving noises coming from the right. Albert's attempted reforms of Society were highly unpopular with what Victoria called the "Fashionables". In her eyes, these represented the so-called "old Royal Family" as compared with the young newcomer from Saxe-Coburg; supported by extravagant, frivolous, immoral sections of the aristocracy, as compared with Victoria's untainted Court. All this hounding by the right-wing "Fashionables" was going on a hundred years and more before Elizabeth II came to the throne. Anti-monarchist propaganda towards the end of Victoria's reign all came from the left or centre: radicals like Sir Charles Dilke or Joseph Chamberlain, or Liberals who voted against the Civil List payments for Queen Victoria's children. Rumours about the Queen and John Brown, however, she believed originated "in elegant drawing-rooms" and with "ill-natured gossip in the higher classes".

In the last four or five years a wave of right-wing dissatisfaction has developed and is still mounting. Anthony Holden quoted a letter in the *Sunday Times* that accused the Monarchy of having "lost direction", of being "over-exposed". Again, modern criticism of royal tax policy came rather more from the better off than the poor. One hears

109

remarks like, "We pay forty per cent income tax, Prince Charles pays twenty-five per cent." This is not the kind of criticism to come from people who are too poor to pay any income tax at all.

Admittedly provoked by Prince Charles himself ("I like stirring things up"), the voices of leading professionals are heard complaining of royal interference. They may not be left-wing or right-wing, but neither have they hitherto been anti-royal. No doubt the Prince of Wales began it with his carbuncular speech, his "giant glass stump" of the Palumbo consortium in Mansion House Square, and his Luftwaffe metaphor of 1 December 1987. The Prince deplored what he saw as "the jostling crowd of office buildings" desecrating St Paul's "like a basket-ball team standing shoulder to shoulder between you and the Mona Lisa. . . . You have, Ladies and Gentlemen, to give this much to the Luftwaffe: when it knocked down our buildings, it didn't replace them with anything more offensive than rubble. *We* did that." Modern planning, said the Prince wittily, was "the continuation of war by other means" — a reversed reference to Karl von Clausewitz's famous definition of war as "the continuation of diplomacy by other means".

The Prince, indeed, has a gift for smothering ugly modern buildings in ridicule. The Birmingham Central Library is "like a place where books are incinerated, not kept". Because some buildings house word-processors they need not look like word-processors. The National Theatre is "more like a bunker than a palace". Prince Charles has been likened to John Ruskin. Certainly the great Victorian prophet of beauty and truth in architecture would have approved of the Prince's crusade. But recently the professionals have reversed the insults, and Prince Charles is in danger of becoming the monstrous carbuncle on the elegant, much-loved face of the RIBA. If he lived in a glass house it would be extremely hazardous for him to throw what he calls "the proverbial royal brick through the inviting plate glass of pompous professional pride". Even though he lives in St James's Palace his courageous operations are not free from risk. Nor do they go unappreciated, according to an opinion poll conducted by Gallup for BBC TV early in November 1992. Which individual, rather than political party, should run the country in a Cabinet of National Recovery? Prince Charles was appointed Secretary of State for the Environment.

The respectable classes have also shown signs of turning against some royal activities. The Yorks before their separation were seen at a theatre with a "Madam". Prince Edward was said to have "demeaned" the British Monarchy in 1987 with a television film, *The Grand Knock-Out Tournament*, and to have begun the decline and fall.* Even the Queen was suddenly put under literary arrest and sentenced to three columns in Peter McKay's page of the *Evening Standard*. Her Majesty's alleged crime? She had produced three out of four children whose marriages had gone wrong. It must be, he thought, to some extent her fault.

*A skit on a medieval joust produced by the BBC in aid of the Wildlife Fund, it boasted a professional comedian (Stuart Hall), professional noblemen (Westminster, Roxburghe and Abercorn) and professional royalties (the Yorks, Prince Edward, the Princess Royal, the Duke of Gloucester). At one point the race to be King of the Castle had Anne and Edward splitting their sides. I suppose it would be dangerous to argue that royalty can do absolutely anything provided charity is tacked on. But if you like knock-about farce, there was nothing very much wrong with this.

111

Queen Elizabeth II is the lynch-pin of the whole royal system. To decide whether the Monarchy's survival is likely or unlikely involves some detailed investigation into Her Majesty's chances. Therefore, though she is by far the most significant figure in the whole cast, her entry must be reserved for the last chapter.

Meanwhile, what is the betting that the various suggestions for updating the Monarchy would be acceptable, workable or valuable?

CHAPTER
SIX

Updating the Monarchy

Arthur Scargill, President of the NUM: "I have always said that there should be no monarchy. They should be found reasonable jobs in society, unemployment figures permitting." Peter Blake, pop artist: "I am a royalist. The Queen does her job very well. It's the 20th century that's gone wrong around her."

The Independent, *26 November 1992*

Improbable as it may sound, Queen Mary's guideline was go-ahead: "One must move with the times." Admittedly, as the wife of George V, she was not encouraged to move far. Her skirts were forbidden to move even a few inches above her ankles, as most ladies' skirts did at this time. But she could move her granddaughters, Elizabeth and Margaret Rose, around London's museums and art galleries, giving them a more up-to-date education in history and culture than their governess "Crawfie" could possibly imagine. Their grandfather George V, however, was absolutely "uniform", predictable and unchanging through and through. He was the last of that immovable royal breed. In varying degrees all his descendants have moved with the times. It was just a question of how far, and in what direction.

Before considering the specific changes that have been suggested to Queen Elizabeth II, or that she herself might favour, it will be as well to make an excursion down one particular side-alley. Since the royal turmoil of 1992, there has been some sharp questioning of the times that we live in. Are they the kind of "times" that we should want to move with — or away from? What sort of age is it that seems to prefer a showbiz monarchy to a dignified royal family — even if it sometimes means turning a blind eye to their undignified "antics"? An age that acquiesces in every self-respecting charity insisting on having its own royal patron, so that there can never be too many "Royals" around to fulfil these tasks. In the perceptive words of Kenneth Rose, author of *George V*, the present Monarch has entered Coronation Street and a little of the mystery has gone for ever. That is no doubt the price we are prepared to pay for the Queen's immensely popular walkabouts.

Are we also prepared for a younger generation of the Royal Family who will risk the perils of using mobile telephones for intimate conversations in an age when anything that can be pirated is fair game? The Princess of Wales is said to have been pleased when the existence and preliminary glimpses of the alleged taped mobile telephone conversation between the Prince of Wales and Mrs Camilla Parker Bowles were revealed by the *Daily Mirror* on 10 November 1992. "Camillagate", as it was instantly called, since the Prince had apparently told Camilla she was "loved and adored", had been taped in 1989, just about the same time as "Dianagate". "That makes the balance even," Princess Diana was said to have commented. The Princess may indeed welcome an age of exposure-all-round, but is it good for the Monarchy?

Those who think it is not, who think that it is an unwelcome sign of the times, have a one-off way of updating the Monarchy that is all their own. Let the Monarchy be updated by going backwards — back to a time of fewer romps and more reasonableness; less of a perpetual daily performance and more of the old-fashioned scenario of hard-to-get; less soap and more dignity. Some of these critics, who are of course in a minority, go as far as suggesting a sabbatical year for the whole Royal Family, with the exception of Her Majesty herself. This would give all the younger members a chance to calm down and meet each other only in private rather than on platforms, where partners tend to become sparring partners. Journalists should no longer be able to watch the Princess of Wales indulging in certain kinds of platform-play: lifting her mini skirt, for instance, an extra inch or two above her knees in order to distract attention from her husband's speech when they were on tour. A sabbatical year for royalty would give the media a golden opportunity to deflect the public's prurience and taste for royal gossip — at present disgracefully pandered to and aggravated — into more interesting channels, where it might gradually lose its new-found virulence.

Even without a sabbatical year for all royalty except the Queen, much could be done in a negative sense to improve the Monarchy's image. Many people would agree that as an institution it has become ubiquitous, therefore trivialised. Prince Michael of Kent points out that journalists show less and less interest in the increasing amount of work that all the Royal Family undertake; but if a small girl drops a curtsy to one of them and topples over, it is front-page news.

Prince Charles felt compelled to ask a gathering of editors why they had taken to concentrating on his marital difficulties while virtually ignoring his serious contribution to the national life, for example, his work for the deprived. One answer would be that the editors had to give their readers what they wanted. If their readers had a choice between the sufferings of two unhappy people in a palace and twenty even more unhappy people in the high-rise flats of an inner city, they would always choose the palace. And the *Sun* is very well satisfied with its circulation; it will never turn its baleful beams off royalty as long as a tapped telephone can add a million to its sales. The top men on the *Daily Mirror* have been trained in the same stable, actually on the *Sun*. The only solution, goes this argument by critical monarchists, is simple: if the tabloids won't go away, the Royal Family must do so.

After this one-off pause for meditation and reassessment, continues the argument, the family would return to public life on a new basis, with its profile permanently lower and concentrated on royalty's true realm: namely, the complex trilogy of Britain, the Commonwealth and Europe.

Two immediate objections to the sabbatical year arise. Even though the Queen herself would clearly be exempt, she might feel diminished without the public support of her family. "I have to be seen to be believed," she once said, and she likes to be seen with her family. More than once she has stated specifically her belief in *the* family, which of course includes *her* family. "I am for it," she said at the time of her Silver Wedding, pithily quoting the legendary bishop's reply to someone who asked him what he thought of sin: "I am against it."

A few years later, at her Silver Jubilee in 1977, the Queen introduced the idea of the family being responsible for the success or otherwise of marriage. As we have already seen in Chapter 4, she visualised the partners in a marriage as being firmly bound together, so to speak, by the "web" of their extended families. Much has happened to royal marriages since the date of those remarks. It might be thought that the delicate "web of family relationships" had been irreparably torn by the pressures of the modern world. Since then, three royal marriages have been made and three unmade.

Nevertheless, the Queen would rightly speak up as strongly for the family today as she did sixteen years ago — perhaps even more strongly.

For example, on the afternoon of Friday, 20 November 1992, we saw with a pang the small figure of Her Majesty, in head scarf and wellingtons, standing desolate against the flaming ruins of St George's Hall and the Brunswick Tower in Windsor Castle. Her one consolation, amid all the horror and loss, was the presence of her son, Prince Andrew, Duke of York. *He* would see that everything possible was done to salvage the treasures. And indeed he — looking tough and vigorous to a degree — and all those with whom he was working devotedly in the Castle, made a magnificent job of it.

Beside the Queen's own dependence on her family for practical and moral support, there is another branch of opinion from which protests would arise at a royal sabbatical year. This is the whole powerful world of Charity, within which the Royal Family works to enormous effect.

It must be recognised that an important change has taken place in the last half-century or so. This change has been vividly described by Princess Alice, Duchess of Gloucester, in her fascinating *Memoirs* (1983). When the young Henry, Duke of Gloucester, proposed to her, her father, the Duke of Buccleuch, objected that she would lose her independence. "If I married Prince Henry, I would have to accept that I was a servant of the Country." Nevertheless, she went ahead and married the Prince. Then, having reported that her task as the country's servant had turned out far more arduous than she expected, Princess Alice proceeded to explain why. First, because of the great and tedious increase in security; and second, the equally onerous increase in official functions since the war. Compared with pre-war days, recalls Princess Alice, there were many more such functions, a large number of them dedicated to raising money for charitable causes. At the same time there were far fewer "local dignitaries" with "the time or money" to perform these functions. (And perhaps fewer with the charisma or audience-appeal to do the job.) The extended Royal Family was drafted in to fill the gap. And now that the change in supply has been made, the demand for royalty has increased. There is no going back.

The only possible change was on another front, and that was the change which, in fact, came about dramatically towards the end of 1992.

When members of the Royal Family were invited after the war to step on to a thousand official platforms, and accepted, they stepped forward supported by the Civil List. In other words, the Treasury paid their expenses. In the case of three of these working members of the Royal Family — Princess Alexandra and the Dukes of Kent and Gloucester — the Queen reimbursed the Treasury on their behalf. But the total set-up, like all financial situations, was by no means stable and it was always possible that all Civil List payments to "minor royals" would come to an end some day. In which case they would have to be reimbursed for expenses either by the good causes they served or by the Queen. That day was to dawn, as we shall see, five days after the Great Fire of Windsor.

Meanwhile, a point has been reached in our discussion of that whimsical proposal for a royal sabbatical when it must be superseded by something more probable and practical. The size of the Royal Family is one of the main areas of modern criticism. Is it too big?

Those who say "Yes" generally begin by citing its phenomenal latterday increase in size. From four to forty, in little over forty years, according to Nigel Dempster. There was something rather special, they add, about the royal "Firm", as defined by King George VI: a firm of just four members — the King, the Queen, Princess Elizabeth and Princess Margaret. That was the "Firm" until Prince Philip joined it in 1947. It is interesting to note that at the above date, when Princess Elizabeth and Prince Philip got married, there were at least two other senior members of the Royal Family living: Queen Mary and Prince Henry, Duke of Gloucester, a queen consort and the son of a monarch respectively. Yet King George VI did not see either of them as members of the "Firm".

If we look around Europe today, in the countries where monarchy has survived or been revived, there are more royal families that resemble in numbers King George VI's "Firm" than Queen Elizabeth II's clan. Members of the Spanish royal family, for instance, consist of the King and Queen, their son and two daughters; just five, or seven if you count the King's

119

two sisters. In the Danish royal family we find the Queen and her two sons, the Prince Consort, the Queen's father's late brother's wife, her two sons and the Queen Mother, a total of nine.

If the British Royal Family were reduced to similar proportions, it could again consist of single figures, either seven or nine; alternatively it could be allowed to reach low double figures. Drastically cut down, the Family would include only the Queen, her Consort, the Prince of Wales, his separated wife and their two sons, and the Queen Mother. The two other sons of the Monarch, Prince Andrew and Prince Edward, could also be admitted, to bring the number up to nine. There are people, however, who would prefer to see no one on the list except the Queen, Prince Philip and the heir to the throne. But this austere minority are probably keener on getting rid of the Monarchy altogether — by squeezing it and squeezing it until the pips squeak — than on improving it and making it more manageable. In fact, the majority of monarchists would almost certainly prefer a slightly larger Royal Family than the single figures suggested above. The addition of Prince Andrew's two daughters, Princess Beatrice and Princess Eugénie, the Princess Royal and Princess Margaret would be popular, bringing the total number up to thirteen. And if that number were thought to be unsuitable, we could forget about the two little Princesses (who, after all, correspond only to the Dukes of Gloucester and Kent and Prince Michael — all grandchildren of a sovereign), which would achieve a satisfactory total of eleven.

What are the disadvantages of smaller numbers? The Queen's dependence on her family's help has already been mentioned. Without it, the royal impact on the country would be noticeably diminished. This might not be a bad thing if the impact itself were bad, as it was during the summer of 1992. On the other hand, it would preclude the splendour and richness of the British royal turn-out that people have come to expect. Smaller numbers would almost inevitably go with a simpler way of life. Something more like the Scandinavian and other European monarchies cited above for their relatively small families. Small is beautiful; it is also more homely, less spectacular, and not so bedizened with pageantry: bicycles instead of Aston Martins; bobbies in caps with check bands instead of sentries in busbies to guard the Queen's home; the Opening of Parliament on a dark, rainy Saturday evening when traffic would not be inconvenienced — or the ceremony seen — instead of tiaras, a state coach, the Windsor greys. It would all be a different kind of grey.

These potential changes have been listed here among the *disadvantages* of small, unpretentious royal families. Many people, perhaps twenty-five per cent of monarchists, would nevertheless prefer this kind of royal family. It has come to be known at its best and most traditional as a "Bicycling Monarchy", though a line of royal bicycles parked in the forecourt of Buckingham Palace is not necessary to its realisation. Not that there is anything wrong with bicycles; they are simply being used as symbols for more ordinariness and accessibility, less luxury and Olympian remoteness. The young Queen Victoria's "Carriage Monarchy" made her almost too accessible, for people were always waylaying the Royal Family and shouting cheery greetings into her carriage. It was only when the "Railway Monarchy" developed that

121

the Royal Family could — and still can — make a complete getaway.

Among those who understand the royal system, there is as much difference of opinion about this question of the Royal Family's size as there is among those without any special knowledge. Hugo Vickers, for instance, is an expert who sees the many minor "royals" in an original and favourable light. They are in a sense like the family's "Life Peers", he says, necessary to make the system work. To lose such large numbers of active, usually young members of her clan, would inevitably weaken the Queen's potential. She would be unable to answer all the fresh calls on her time, thereby causing disappointment and criticism.

On the contrary, Martin Charteris, who has been the Queen's most successful private secretary, argues that the Royal Family has become too big for the task it has to perform. That task must include setting an example. Unless the Monarchy is in some way an archetype, it will not survive. And if one examines the problem areas of the modern Monarchy, they will more often be found on the periphery than at the centre. Cut it down to size, and there would be more chance of an archetypal family developing again, as in the 1930s and 1940s.

The present author finds the case for a smaller Royal Family convincing on the whole. As with all things human, however, it might not work out. Unless the press co-operated, the Queen might find herself getting the worst of both worlds. If the circulation war of the tabloids were to continue as it does now, we should have a situation where every third and fourth cousin of the Queen was hounded for every peccadillo, just as before, whereas the fringe "royals" themselves would feel no obligation, no sanctions, to make them behave differently (better) than any of their contemporaries. In other words, though they would no longer be "royal" according to the Queen's fiat, they would still be "royal" according to the tabloids' practice. There have already been examples of such injustices: for instance, when a minor motoring offence committed by a distant relative of the Queen was given totally unfair publicity solely because it was an allegedly "royal" lapse. Such treatment might continue and even increase at the hands of a press desperate for royal gossip. And the archetypal Monarchy would be as far away as ever.

Other areas that are said to be ripe for change mainly involve the Palace and are interwoven. First, the Royal Household. Since time immemorial a sovereign's household has been criticised, mainly for unedifying human reasons, often jealousy. To name only four cases in the last century: Queen Caroline, wife of George IV, was said to have lived with her majordomo; so also was the Duchess of Kent, Queen Victoria's mother; and both Queen Adelaide, wife of William IV, and Vicky, eldest daughter of Queen Victoria and wife of the German Emperor, were said to have lived with their court chamberlains. Queen Elizabeth II does not have to refute or live with such malignities, but accusations on a different level continue to multiply. Here are two of the most sweeping examples, both appearing in the press on the same day, 26 November 1992.

The *Independent* asked a selection of famous people, "Where does the Monarchy go from here?", and printed thirty replies, eighteen pro-monarchy, nine anti-monarchy and three half-and-half. In the last group, Nigel Dempster, the *Daily Mail* diarist, hit out at the weaknesses of the Royal Family: too many of them and too ill-served. "The weaknesses of their staff — lick-spittles and flatterers — is going to bring them down, if it hasn't already." Stephen Glover, political commentator of the *Evening Standard*, thought that the Queen did not necessarily oppose changes but did not know how to bring them about: "Rarely has an English monarch been surrounded by advisers so ill-fitted to their duties."

At the start of my rebuttal it must be pointed out that the Sovereign's chief advisers and main line of defence against the eternal tabloids — for Stephen Glover says the tabloids will never lay off — are the Prime Minister, the Cabinet Secretary and the Queen's private secretary, Sir Robert Fellowes. The Queen can also call in any elder statesman or "wise man" she needs, as she did with Lord ("Rab") Butler over Prince Charles's education. People will have their own views about the first mentioned, who is inevitably a political partisan. But the present private secretary has wisdom born of experience, a quality that the Queen sets much store by and herself possesses to an outstanding degree. He is shrewd, loyal and devoted, absolutely free from affectation, pomposity, or self-importance. True, he is a benchmark for the class and type that critics of the Royal Household particularly dislike. His father was in charge of the Sandringham estate and he himself is married to Lady Jane Spencer, sister of the Princess of Wales. He does indeed belong to the category of quasi-hereditary private secretaries and other top courtiers, of whom examples exist in this century and the last, many of them distinguished. There were the Ponsonbys, the Bigges, the Colvilles, the

Adeanes and the Spencers, some of whom have been mentioned already. It must not be forgotten that Lord Stamfordham (born Arthur Bigge, a good English but not shiningly aristocratic name) was the man who invented the title "House of Windsor" for the Royal Family. Anti-German hysteria had forced King George V to change the family name in 1917 from the German title it was deemed to possess — whether Saxe-Coburg-Gotha, Wettin, Wipper or whatever. The Kaiser made fun of the change to Windsor by saying that he was going to a performance of "The Merry Wives of Saxe-Coburg-Gotha". Had he but known that "Wipper" was one of the possible titles, he might have assumed there were as many perverts in Cousin Georgie's Court as in his own.

If Robert Fellowes can be described as a type of quasi-hereditary private secretary, that may not be a bad thing for an hereditary monarch. Although he says with emphasis that "There is no courtier class", you might say that he himself is the "courtier class" personified: a Guards officer, in the City, connected by family ties with the Court; upper class. Yet he stands out because of the growing rarity of his type. The helpful and highly intelligent press secretary, Charles Anson, has come from the Foreign Office, No. 10 Downing Street and the City. There has been a private secretary from Australia, Sir William Heseltine, and another private secretary from the Civil Service, Sir Philip Moore, as the Palace will proudly tell you. However, there has been criticism that such appointments are not more socially representative, for every institution must change or be chopped.

Another criticism is the supposed existence of anti-feminism at Court. The *locus classicus* of anti-feminism in the Palace is the career of Mrs Michael Wall. It is said that after serving for years, latterly as assistant private secretary, she was never offered the top job: chief secretary to the Queen. In fact, Mrs Wall herself has said that she never wanted the job, involving as it did long tours away from home and the possible need to deal with foreign paparazzi. The case of the critics is not proven either way, though there are definitely not enough top women. There never are.

John Grigg is still an enthusiastic guide to other possible changes. For years he has valiantly pressed the claims of the New Commonwealth at Court: the need for black faces in the upper reaches of the royal secretariat. Sir Robert Fellowes gives assurances that as soon as the right man or woman applies, they will be welcomed. To make a mistake that ended in recriminations and a sudden retirement would be even worse for Commonwealth harmony than making no attempt at all. And how many black faces are found at the top of industry or banking? Nevertheless, the Palace should set an example.

The apparent conviction in the press and elsewhere that the Royal Household is congenitally racist may well be a relic of an old Victorian controversy. Queen Victoria firmly believed that her Household criticised her Indian servants on racist grounds, while her fair-minded doctor, Sir James Reid, as firmly denied it.

Again, the quarrels of Edward VIII with his Household may also have left a legacy of general prejudice. After the Abdication he warned his brother, King George VI, to cling to his "weekends" as being the only defence against the "strangle grip of Buckingham Palace and its officials!!" The only "official" who may be said to have exerted a stranglehold on his Sovereign was George V's doctor, Lord Dawson of Penn. Whereas Dawson famously announced on the wireless (not yet the radio) that the King's life was "moving peacefully towards its close", it had actually been propelled along the terminal road by an injection, said to have been in the jugular.

John Grigg ingeniously proposes to solve the first problem — that of possible racism — by establishing two separate secretariats. One would be for the Queen's home affairs, the other for the Commonwealth, in which blacks would be well represented. The weakness of this plan seems to be a danger of confusion and overlapping. If it had already been in existence during 1992, we can be sure that a malign fate would have arranged for some of Her Majesty's Commonwealth engagements to be accidentally slotted into the very same weeks as important events at home, to the fury of all concerned.

In any case, the changes that loom ahead are likely to be far more extensive than those represented by the idea of two secretariats. A factor that will be dealt with later in this chapter — the payment of the Queen's new taxes — is bound to introduce novel and complex work at the Palace. So would the suggested addition of a press officer from the ranks of journalism to help cope with any new attempts to solve the problem of "privacy". And the growing importance of Europe, in which the Queen will play a real part, increases the prospect of change. Unusually large crowds turned out for the state visit to Germany of the Queen and Prince Philip in October 1992. "A queen", an official explained, "was always more of an attraction than just another president."*

*Daily Telegraph, 20 October 1992.

The German press commented on the Queen's "calming and clear-cut language", at a time when Anglo-German economic relations were disturbing and confused. "I am convinced that the governments and peoples of Britain and Germany", the Queen had said, "can and will work together to build a community to meet the challenge of the new Europe." She and her Consort were to make their own contribution: they attended a moving ecumenical service of reconciliation in Dresden's Kreuzkirche, where the Bishop of Coventry, Simon Barrington-Ward, preached on the theme, "Blessed are the peacemakers". It was indeed as peacemakers that the British royal pair paid their memorable visit to Bonn, Berlin, Dresden, Leipzig and Potsdam.

Then why not solve all the problems, great and small, in one fell swoop? Make the Monarchy, as suggested twenty years and more ago, a Department of State. No more arguments about the Royal Household. No more need of specific pleas for black faces. The Monarchy would be run from Whitehall, under Parliament, exactly like the Departments of Health or Defence or Trade and Industry. There is one simple but fatal objection: the Queen would not have it at any price.

Both the Queen and the Prince of Wales deeply cherish their human relationships, the Queen with her tenants in the Duchy of Lancaster, the Prince with his in the Duchy of Cornwall. The tenant farmers and others, says the Prince, like to look on themselves as part of the family. How much more must the Queen value and depend on her personal household? She rightly has a great deal of symbolising, representing and personification in her life: she symbolises representing and personification in her life: she symbolises the nation's history; she represents the people's aspirations; and she personifies the country's unity in diversity. What she also needs is an inner ring of people close to her, not a Civil Service machinery, however efficient, to mediate her duty. With all its merits, that machinery is inappropriate for performing in the Queen's Household. What the Queen does require in her staff is character as well as efficiency and brains. Charles Anson, for instance, makes a remarkable impression of calm even in the most disturbing circumstances. On a certain day in July 1992, he was interrupted while conducting an interview in the Palace. When he returned, he apologised for leaving his visitor. "I'm so sorry for keeping you waiting. We've had an intruder." The intruder was Darryl Marcus, who had scaled the Palace wall but was picked up as soon as he reached the building.

Whatever changes are brought about in the Royal Household owing to changes in the Queen's work, they will have to be mediated by human beings she knows and trusts. We must not forget Queen Victoria's reaction, at the age of twenty, when "they" tried to remove some of her ladies-in-waiting because of a change of government. "I was calm but very decided," she wrote to Lord Melbourne, her former prime minister, "and I think you would have been pleased to see my composure and great firmness. The Queen of England will not submit to such trickery." After forty years of devoted service, Elizabeth II could say the same kind of thing. She will not be transformed into a machine, to be programmed by bureaucrats along with a thousand other departmental computers.

Another aspect of the Monarchy in which changes have been recommended is that of deference, ceremony and the honours system.

It is true that the present age of *fin de siècle* cynicism cannot be one in which deference flourishes. Less deference is currently found in other institutions beside the Monarchy. There has been far less "cap-touching" since the war. Bishops of the Roman Catholic Church used to be saluted by the faithful with a genuflection and a kiss on their amethyst ring. Today if a senior citizen of the diocese forgets the present custom of a simple handshake and dives for the ring, the episcopal hand will be kindly but firmly withdrawn.

The Monarchy must always be a special case, since it is the country itself, as a totality, that people are saluting when they enter or leave Her Majesty's presence. At the beginning of an interview with a Scandinavian monarch like Queen Margrethe II of Denmark, the equivalent of "Ma'am" is used, though not again during the interview. Sometimes, though, she is addressed in the third person; at other times simply as "you". On leaving the Danish royal presence, visitors take one or two steps backward and then walk out normally. They are instructed before the interview not to be too deferential — for instance, by bowing too low.

Deference (though not respect) for Queen Elizabeth II has already undergone the same kind of diminution. In the days before these changes, British queens, including Victoria and Elizabeth II, had to watch (and try not to laugh) as their ministers mistakenly crawled forward into the presence on their knees, or cannoned into occasional tables as they correctly but clumsily walked out backwards. Today all this innocent fun is over: no hand-kissing — young Queen Victoria's hand was said to be "remarkably soft" — and just two or three steps backward before turning round to make an exit; no kneeling except to be knighted; otherwise only the instruction to "bow from the neck". This may sound a little too much like "hang from the neck", but, apart from that, it should be acceptable. The present author has no objection to curtsying or even kneeling, if unexpectedly required to do so — like the American visitor to the House of Lords who, on hearing Lord Hailsham, the Lord Chancellor, greet his brother across the lobby, "Neil!", promptly fell on her knees. Many people, however, feel that the process of cutting down on royal deference has not yet gone far enough.

The next step, therefore, might be to limit the bowing and curtsying (there is no more "bowing and *scraping*" now that people do not kneel) to the Queen and her Consort, the Queen Mother and the heir to the throne, once he or she has reached the age of eighteen. This is to prevent unnecessary deference, as distinct from respect towards royal children, which cannot be good for them or us.*

It is important to recognise that deference and respect for the Monarchy are not the same thing. You cannot have too much respect, whereas deference is a frill or trimming that, when overdone, can destroy the perfection of dignity, style and taste. Respect, on the contrary, is a climate in which the Monarchy cannot fail to survive. Returning to the Mylius case

*When George VI came to the throne, the two Princesses were told to stop curtsying to their parents, but to keep it up with their grandmother Queen Mary, I suspect on her instructions. On her death-bed she reprimanded the doctor for preparing to leave her bedroom face first: "I'm not dead yet!"

of 1910, a remarkable letter was received by the republican journalist from an equally republican friend in Paris. "The only way to deal with the British Monarchy", he wrote to Mylius, "is to cut away 'respect'. As soon as the people cease to respect it, it is done for." And vice versa: as long as it is respected, it will not be overthrown.

There is a good case also for modernising the Monarchy through a reform of the honours list. In theory the Queen is the "fount of honour", but in practice the vast business of political patronage is in the hands of the Prime Minister. It is suggested that all honours should be decided by a commission, perhaps headed by the Queen. At present, she merely gives her informal approval of the lists so that, as Antony Jay says, at least the recipients have the satisfaction of knowing that they have not been black-balled by Her Majesty.

As for ceremonial, this inevitably becomes simpler as the years go by. In the old days it would have been thought cheese-paring to recycle state bunting or red carpets. Today this is the rule. Documents issued by the Palace to explain some new move, such as the separation of the Prince and Princess of Wales, are written on both sides of the paper. And when the Queen begins paying income tax (a change to be considered in a moment), she may not be able to afford certain ceremonial uniforms which hitherto she has paid for herself. Some dramatic or striking events in the national calendar — Trooping the Colour, the Opening of Parliament, the service on Maundy Thursday, the Garter procession, the Cenotaph — are of their nature ceremonial. People would be loath to abandon such scenes of beauty, embedded in so much of the nation's history. And so the next discussion must occupy a wider stage: how genuine is the alleged public demand for a monarchy more nearly resembling the majority of monarchies in Europe?

To begin with, the demand is by no means universal. Nigel Nicolson, son of Harold Nicolson and himself a distinguished writer, says: "We don't want a cheap monarchy." Andrew Roberts, much acclaimed young author of *The Holy Fox*, Lord Halifax's biography, writes scornfully of the possible "Scandinavianisation" of the British Monarchy, demanding instead what he calls a "New Deal" both for Queen and country, consisting of a return to some of the best pre-Victorian values. By this he means a distinction between the Royal Family and the Monarchy, respect for royalty's privacy and an end to vulgarisation. Professor Cannadine thought (on television) that if the Royal Family survived, it might be "trivialised" into a "Monaco Monarchy", which he rightly would not welcome.

These strictures, while well deserved, do not rule out the possibility of learning something from the smaller European monarchies. Denmark and Holland, for instance, both allow direct access by press and people to their popular queens. Queen Margrethe II of Denmark gives interviews on the first Monday of the month, seeing up to sixty people. She is known to conduct the press interviews brilliantly. With gossip-columnists that are kindly and a crown that is adaptable, Queen Margrethe can walk into a shop unnoticed and lead a relatively normal life. Accessibility, of course, to the Queen of five million people is a different proposition from accessibility to the Queen of nearly fifty-five million. Nevertheless, if something on Danish lines could be the subject of experiments here, despite our intrusive press, the position of Elizabeth II could be strengthened.

By design, the Spanish monarch, King Juan Carlos, has a very small court. (The population of Spain is thirty-eight million, two-thirds of Britain's.) The Queen of Spain has no ladies-in-waiting at all, a fact that aroused the opposition of some *grandes dames* belonging to Madrid's high society. So they tackled the Queen. "Ma'am," they said, "we do think you ought to have some ladies-in-waiting — it must be very difficult for you to manage without." Perhaps they would not have minded filling those posts themselves. "No, I don't think I need a lady-in-waiting, thank you," replied the Queen, "but if you know of a good lady's *maid*, I should be very glad to hear from you."

The disadvantage of a small court is its weakness in organisation. It is hard to plan ahead or to be sure of plans being carried through. "The advantage", says one who knows the Spanish royal family well, "is that the King is really exposed directly to his people, and that's the role which he feels happiest in."

Incidentally, the remarkable nature of the Spanish monarchy's renaissance after so many years of opprobrium has not always been adequately recognised. It is generally accepted, for instance, that it was the King who saved democracy by pre-empting a military coup and smartly ordering the army back to barracks.

A relatively simple style of living characterises both the Spanish and Danish courts. Neither monarch possesses great personal wealth, Queen Margrethe being left with a private income of about £100,000 after she has paid salaries and so on out of her state budget. Nor is the British Monarchy itself given to luxurious living, at least since George IV and with the later exception of Edward VII. William IV wanted to avoid the expense of a traditional Coronation altogether, while Queen Victoria handed down her children's clothes and enjoyed living the simple life in a plain little villa on the Balmoral estate, as a change from Scottish baronial. King George V far preferred York Cottage to Sandringham House, and King George VI was positively averse to red carpets except when really necessary. Neither Queen Elizabeth II nor the future King Charles III would have any trouble, temperamentally, with a touch of "Scandinavianisation" — except possibly with the word.

Accessibility is already practised by the whole British Royal Family in the form of walkabouts; and "direct exposure to the people" through audiences, as cultivated by the European monarchies, would surely have been tried here already but for the ratpack. Prince Charles once said he wanted people to follow him, not through personal dominance but through attraction, like a kind of Pied Piper. If only he could attract the ratpack and persuade them to follow him to Mount Lochnagar, where, like the Brunswick rats, they would vanish inside, never to be seen again.

To sum up: the British Monarchy can learn something from the foreign versions, chiefly in the way of accessibility. Has not Prince Charles himself criticised the insular British for being unwilling to learn from abroad? However, there is one aspect of "Scandinavianisation" that would immensely enhance the popularity of our monarchy, but which at present is known only to a tiny minority. The learned, charming and beautiful Margrethe II has written and published her memoirs. Recounted in the first person, through a ghost, they were finished in 1989 and have since been translated into English. If only Elizabeth II would do the same, in her own pithy style.

At the end of the Danish Queen's attractive, well-illustrated volume, we know what she feels about growing up as a royal, marriage, religious faith, the monarchy, happiness, painting, needlework, the press, life and death. There is space to quote only two of her opinions verbatim, but these few words tell us more about a modern monarch — her self-confidence and her self-criticism — than all the print-mountains piled up by royal watchers. On the press she writes:

> I am well aware of the press's favourite subjects.
> No. 1: my husband's pronunciation of Danish [he is French]. . . .
> No. 2: "The Queen smokes!" . . .
> No. 3: our acquaintances. It is largely the tabloids who appoint certain people our "acquaintances". Both my husband, my sons and I know and associate with many people the press do not know about, thank heavens. . . .

In the last self-revelatory chapter on "Life and Death," she writes: "I have not grown 'milder' with age. I rather believe I have become sharper and I must take great care not to become really bossy. . . ."

We know from the film, *Elizabeth R*, that our Queen keeps a diary, though a short one, "which is the only way I can write". If Her Majesty felt like publishing her memoirs, written in that same brief, accurate style, what a welcome they would receive. After all, Queen Victoria published her

Leaves from a Journal of our Life in the Highlands during her lifetime. It was much acclaimed — except by her eldest son and one or two of the Household.

*   *   *

For a variety of reasons, including the recession — lost jobs, lost homes, the prosperous becoming poor, the poor becoming hopeless — criticism of the Queen's untaxed income began to assume unpleasant proportions in 1992. Her wealth was again being "wildly exaggerated" as in 1971–2; but whereas at that date the vast sum was said to amount to between £50 million and £100 million, twenty years later the supposed figure, even more "wildly exaggerated", had shot up to £6.5 billion. "Absolute crap!" said Prince Edward. The true sum was probably still in the lower millions, the miscalculation having made no allowance whatever for expenditure. The tabloids developed a damaging refrain: the Queen was the wealthiest woman in Britain and "one of the richest people in the world". Why should the homeless contribute towards the "antics" of the Queen's daughters-in-law? continued the angry chant.

There were random reports during the summer of 1992 that the Queen was going to pay income tax. Hopes were momentarily fixed on the Prime Minister's annual visit to Balmoral, but nothing seemed to come of it. Autumn holidays passed into a sad November. There was no sign of an end to the recession. Her Majesty's Opposition took a twenty-three per cent lead over Her Majesty's Government in the polls and Her Majesty herself had returned from Balmoral to Windsor Castle with no problems apparently nearer to solution. Everything seemed "weary, stale, flat, and unprofitable", our England "an unweeded garden".

Suddenly, in the course of exactly one week, the whole scene had been revolutionised.

Up to that Friday, 20 November 1992, people were not putting much money on an immediate recovery in the Crown's popularity. "Something like a royal wedding might do it," said an experienced journalist, "or even a royal christening." But short of such unlikely events, he could see little hope. Nor could he foresee the Princess Royal's wedding in December.

It was not to be a royal jubilation that triggered the change, but a royal catastrophe. Such is the paradoxical manner in which human affairs progress.

On "Black Friday" Windsor Castle was as usual under repair. With shock and sorrow we saw our silver screens turn to an awful gold in the light of St George's Hall, the Queen's private chapel and the Brunswick Tower, all of them on fire. (Incidentally, to repair an old building seems the surest way to destroy it. Towards the end of the same month, Vienna's splendid Hofburg Palace, also under repair, went up in flames.) Little did we guess, however, that the Castle's tragic châtelaine, who had earlier spent hectic hours helping to rescue works of art from the threatened buildings and now stood silhouetted against the conflagration, was a royal phoenix soon to rise from the ashes. But the phoenix was not to enjoy an unhindered flight upwards.

At first, indeed, there was an overwhelming rush of sympathy for the unfortunate Queen. "She didn't need *this*," people said. She had watched the devastation of her childhood home, herself "devastated", as Prince Andrew put it on television. The Luftwaffe with its flying bombs had failed to catch the young sisters, Elizabeth and Margaret, when chasing them in the Great Park as if with deliberate intent, or to demolish the grey walls of their fortress and air-raid shelter. But now the destruction which had eluded the Luftwaffe was being achieved by some miracle of modern science, home-grown. The Queen's calm fortitude yet obviously deep distress (she was to lose her voice through strain and cold) touched all hearts. If a poll had been taken on the Monarchy, yes or no, that day, the optimum yes vote of ninety-five per cent would certainly have been registered.

On the very next day, the unlucky phoenix was pushed back towards the hot ashes by Cabinet ministers who had intended to step in as knights in shining armour. Before the cultural, artistic and historical aspects of the calamity were even half understood, let alone the personal anguish of the Queen, the public were asked to fix their minds on the *cost*.

The well-meaning Peter Brooke, Secretary of State for National Heritage, announced his Government's intention to foot the whole repair bill, which might be as much as £60 million. The announcement was little short of disastrous in its timing.

The royal phoenix at once stopped rising skywards as an almighty clamour broke out, virtually against the Monarchy. The Government, who so self-righteously was coming to the Castle's aid, was in fact pledging £60 million of the taxpayers' money. This was at once understood. It was also understood within a few hours that there was no redress. All the great show-pieces — Windsor Castle, Buckingham Palace, the Palace of Holyroodhouse, Hampton Court, the Tower of London — were the proud possessions of the nation. As such they were the taxpayers' financial responsibility, taxpayers who surveyed the inexorable legal position with mounting bitterness. Though Windsor Castle was the Queen's favourite home, they understood, she was neither going to contribute to its restoration, *nor did she pay income tax*. Two or three people on BBC's *Question Time* were soon suggesting that until there were no more underfunded hospitals and schools in the country, Windsor Castle should take a back seat. In which case the country's finest historical monument and image of its past glories would have remained unrepaired for ever.

Next day, 22 November, was a day of Sunday newspapers and fiery recriminations.

Then, without warning, on Monday the 23rd, the wind changed again, and again the flames of popular wrath died down. It was the occasion of a Guildhall luncheon to celebrate the fortieth year of Her Majesty's reign. There was no lack of irony. The Queen's host, the Lord Mayor of London, was clad in brilliant ermine from head to foot, the Queen in darkest navy. It seemed to be the nearest that Her Majesty could get to the forbidden black. The television lights contributed a macabre glow of their own, giving the navy a veneer of rusty green.

In a small, hoarse voice, though a voice still as firm as her atrocious cold would allow, the Queen made the first completely unforgettable speech of her reign. John Grigg in 1957 (then Lord Altrincham) had urged the young Elizabeth II to learn to make speeches that her people would always remember. Thirty-five years later, the ghastly year 1992 had brought forth the first.

It will always be known as the *annus horribilis* speech

— the speech marking, as she said, a horrible year. Her listeners quickly realised that it was a coded message to say that she herself was listening to a wider audience. All institutions, she assured them, the Monarchy and City of London not least, must expect to face criticism; but let it be tempered with "a touch of gentleness, good humour and understanding". In those conditions, criticism could become "an engine for change".

Everyone understood that the year was "horrible" for the speaker because of her family troubles, the Windsor Castle débâcle (which she mentioned), the recession at home and the war in what used to be Yugoslavia. It was also the first time that most people could remember Her Majesty speaking of "criticism" and "change" in the same approving breath. And this was quite natural, since she had never done so before in public. When Queen Victoria had been criticised for her life-style and asked to change it (from melancholy seclusion to visible public service), she had sent an angry anonymous letter to *The Times* and privately threatened to abdicate. Only the most cynical listener could believe that Elizabeth II's unique acceptance of criticism would not result in change of some kind.

Nevertheless, the fifth day of this extraordinary royal week, Tuesday 23 November, showed no signs of that gentleness and understanding, or even of the touch of good humour for which the Queen had pleaded, though no doubt the *Sun* as usual thought that it had all along been very funny. With the coarsest possible brutality, it asked her "Maj" to stop addressing its British readers in Latin and, without a blush, offered its own thoroughly English headline for the Queen's *annus horribilis* speech: "One's

141

Bum Year". Anthony Holden supposed that the Queen was wooing the tabloids. "The Queen's remarks at the Guildhall lunch", he wrote in the *Spectator* on 28 November, "seemed to be aimed at attracting sympathy from the tabloid press." If so, Her Majesty must have been rapidly disillusioned.

In fact, the Queen was more likely to have been addressing the critical members of the middle classes, whose unexpected activity we have noted in the previous chapter. The Queen informed us in her Guildhall speech that the term "*annus horribilis*" had been suggested to her by "a sympathetic correspondent". This word "correspondent" surely meant letter-writer, not journalist, one of the 200–300 people who write to the Queen every day.*

In any case, the Great Fire of Windsor, like the Great Fire of London, was to burn up pests from the past and make way for a healthier future. In seventeenth-century London the plague was finally eradicated by the flames; in twentieth-century Windsor the flames caused an end to the growing social trauma of a relatively tax-free Monarchy.

On Wednesday, 25 November 1992, only two days after the Queen's *annus horribilis* speech, John Major, the Prime Minister, announced in Parliament, at the Queen's wish, that she and the Prince of Wales would pay income tax. (Hitherto the Prince had made voluntary contributions to the Treasury from his Duchy of Cornwall assets: at first fifty per cent, then, after his marriage, twenty-five per cent.) From April 1993 onwards, the whole Royal Family would be paying income tax. At the same time, only three members of her

*Her correspondent turned out to be the distinguished Sir Edward Ford, a former assistant private secretary at the Palace.

family would continue on the Civil List, that is, drawing their expenses from the taxpayer. Those three would be the Queen herself, Prince Philip and Queen Elizabeth the Queen Mother. The Queen would pay out of her own private income what were formerly the Civil List expenses of the Princess Royal, Prince Andrew, Prince Edward and Princess Alice of Gloucester. As for the Duke of Gloucester, the Duke of Kent and Princess Alexandra, the Queen was already, as has been said, reimbursing the Treasury for its Civil List payments to those three. The Queen had cut the knot herself, it appeared, rather than adopt the "voluntary" action once forced upon her great-great-grandmother, Queen Victoria, by Prime Minister Peel.

The *annus horribilis* had indeed become an *annus mirabilis* — the poet John Dryden's name for the year of London's Great Fire and the City's miraculous recovery from it. Here was Elizabeth II deliberately forgoing one of the Sovereign's most valuable historical prerogatives. That she was fulfilling the will of her people in renouncing this right not to pay tax seemed obvious from the reception given to her decision, beginning with the warm welcome declared by both party leaders, John Major and John Smith. *The Times*, as part of the Murdoch empire, was not hysterically grateful, but its restrained approval was none the less clear. "It was a response to a chasm of distrust", announced its first leader, "that has been dug between people and palace by junior royalty and competitive newspapers." The caption ran: "Concessions by the Queen should heal the wounds of Windsor."

The *Financial Times* also welcomed the Queen's action, but only in its third leader, after those on GATT and local taxation. It asked whether "the minor members of the royal family" would now stop being pestered by the press, since the taxpayer had ceased to fund them? The answer from the *FT* was "no". And would extreme left-wing politicians no longer criticise the Queen's wealth? The answer was again "no". That the *FT* had made no mistake was proved by the characteristic reaction of Dennis Skinner, the "Beast of [MP for] Bolsover": "It's a fix."

Amusingly, the *Mirror* and *Sun*, two of the leading "competitive newspapers", each claimed the Queen's decision as their own exclusive triumph. "*So Welcome,*" commented the *Mirror*; "Well done, Ma'am! You obviously read the *Daily Mirror* . . . and take notice of what we say. We led the way in demanding that you pay tax and that the minor royals should stop sponging off the taxpayer." The *Sun*, though approving, stuck to its self-consciously rude manner: "About Time Too, Ma'am! 90 per cent of *Sun* readers urged the Queen to fork out . . . *We Said It First*. The *Sun* was the first with the news that the Queen was preparing to pay tax."

Even Dr Edgar Wilson of the *Republican Magazine* was made happy by the Queen's financial sacrifice. Far from seeing it as likely to strengthen the Monarchy, he gleefully interpreted it as the beginning of the end. "Today they pay tax, tomorrow they'll travel by bus and bicycle. The day after nobody will notice as they fade from the scene like the smile on the face of the Cheshire cat."

Dr Wilson forgets that the Cheshire cat existed only in Wonderland. In the real world the smiles of the Royal Family are likely to grow ever broader as they shed their outdated prerogatives.

In the light of this taxed royal future, it would be valuable to know what the Prince of Wales thinks about it all. Incidentally, it was the Prince, rather than the *Daily Mirror* and *Sun*, who actually convinced the Queen that this was the right step forward for a modern monarchy. Speaking over two months before the seven November days that were to re-shape the Monarchy, the Prince nevertheless was already looking forward into a changed future. He described misunderstandings about the Crown's financial situation as "enormous". There were two areas where royal wealth was exaggerated: financial assets and personal possessions. "I think it is time", he said, "to rationalise the whole thing — introduce a much neater arrangement that people can understand."

The "neater" arrangement to which the Prince referred was a return of the Crown Estate, which had been surrendered by the Queen at the beginning of her reign, to the Monarchy. "The Crown Estate should be used in its entirety to run the whole royal operation."

And if the Queen were asked to pay taxes, there would have to be changes in other directions. "Other members of the Royal Family", added the Prince, "should be allowed to take a job when they want." (One supposes the Prince included himself among the "other members".) "Like all things in life", he continued, "nothing is ever simple. There is never something for nothing, and if they want to take away something on one side, then there are other areas that will have to be released." In other words, if the Queen is to pay taxes "like the rest of us", her family will need to earn their living "like the rest of us".

In the new dispensation, now a fact of history, the Prince

clearly envisages a creative opportunity for him to develop the Duchy of Cornwall both commercially and culturally. At present (February 1993) the Duchy is run by a management office; the Treasury controls the whole thing. If it were regularly taxed (up to April 1993 the Duke of Cornwall — Prince Charles — will have made a financial contribution to the Treasury of twenty-five per cent, as already explained), the Prince would expect to run the Duchy himself. But, "the moment you start doing something yourself, people will complain we are using our name, etc., to make money. I want to go into manufacturing — but there'd be an outcry! I think it is better to do the things ourselves than to sell the land to the highest bidder and cause some appalling development. But the moment you start doing it yourself, issuing a challenge . . . then all hell breaks loose!" The Prince laughs heartily. The prospect of the new dispensation by no means depresses him. He is in tearing spirits — tearing away the obstacles and obstructions to a new age.

Unfortunately, the dramatic November days, during which a royal home was partially destroyed and royal taxation totally transformed, were not to bring the sensational events of 1992 to an end. The restoration of Windsor Castle might make it better than ever, as indeed the Queen hoped, but the marriage of the Prince and Princess of Wales was not to be repaired. The country was to learn this, to its sorrow, only nineteen days after the Windsor fire.

On Wednesday, 9 December 1992, John Major made a 161-word announcement in Parliament, from which the following extracts have proved to be of consuming interest:

It is announced from Buckingham Palace that, with regret, the Prince and Princess of Wales have decided to separate. Their Royal Highnesses have no plans to divorce and their constitutional positions are unaffected. This decision [arrived at within the last couple of weeks] has been reached amicably, and they will both continue to participate fully in the upbringing of their children.

The children's first separated Christmas holiday was indeed shared between both parents, Prince William and Prince Harry spending the first part with their father at Sandringham, the second with their mother in the Caribbean. The message continued:

The Queen and the Duke of Edinburgh, though saddened, understand and sympathise with the difficulties that have led to the decision. Her Majesty and His Royal Highness particularly hope that the intrusions into the privacy of the Prince and Princess may now cease. They believe that a degree of privacy and understanding is essential if Their Royal Highnesses are to provide a happy and secure upbringing for their children. . . .

Privacy, however, remains a problem. On 4 January 1993, a serried battery of cameras was photographing Princess Diana and her children in the sea at Nevis at the invitation of the Princess herself, to ensure subsequent privacy.

The widespread reaction to the separation statement was one of sadness and sympathy, but not surprise. Edward Heath, the Tory ex-Prime Minister, called it "one of the saddest announcements made by a prime minister in modern times". The press agreed it was "the end of a fairytale". There were loud "hear hears" from Members of Parliament when privacy was mentioned. That the timing was right seemed to be the general view. Better to "get the whole thing out of the way in *annus horribilis*", with the Princess Royal's wedding as a cheerful epilogue, rather than let the miseries spill over into 1993.

At the same time the public's questions began. How could the Princess be crowned Queen when separated? *Two* royal processions into Westminster Abbey? It might be constitutional but it was not sense. Anyway, it had been tried out by Queen Caroline in the nineteenth century with farcical results. And supposing Charles and Diana later decided to divorce? At this point the pundits parted company. Dr Edward Norman, the church historian, was reported as saying, "Divorce is against canon law. That would be a case for abdication." Lord St John of Fawsley, on the contrary, did not think divorce was a constitutional problem; remarriage might turn out to be one, though there again it could prove soluble.

These are questions for the future (and for further discussion in the next chapter). On 12 December, only three days after the separation announcement of her brother and sister-in-law, the Princess Royal managed to give their mother's horrible year a happy ending by uniting herself to Commander Tim Laurence in Crathie Church at Balmoral. The press had to go to Scotland to rediscover the meaning of "privacy" as it used to be understood. A *Times* journalist, Tom Rhodes, one of 200 others converging on Crathie for the wedding, reported "a silence to rival that of the Mafia in the face of a media invasion". Questioned by Rhodes near the gates of Balmoral, an estate worker replied stonily: "We never talk about Her Majesty and I hope we never will."

*   *   *

We should now be able to see the events of November and December 1992 in the light — or darkness — of the Monarchy's future. Swept along by the wind of taxation, other forms of "updating" can no longer be regarded as merely cosmetic. Will they all combine to strengthen the throne? Or are they milestones on the road to a republic?

CHAPTER
SEVEN

The "Magic of Survival"

The Queen's reign has on the whole been a very good one so far, and it could yet become great. But the chances of its doing so depend upon further fruitful evolution, rather than rigid adherence to existing routines.

John Grigg, The Monarchy Revisited, *1992 (Contemporary Papers)*

"I think this family has survived through the prayers of the people." That was the belief of Princess Margaret in June 1992.* Put in less interesting language, the Princess's feelings were that the people themselves have been responsible for the long-term royal survival. It was the people who wished for it, voted for it in countless polls, took pride and pleasure in it, argued about improvements in it and prayed for it.

Throughout the years, this had been the climate — by and large a mild one. But with *annus horribilis* came pockets of republican weather. Obviously if these pockets developed, they could threaten the Monarchy's survival. But would they so develop? Towards the end of the horrible year there

*Private letter. At the moment that this letter was received, a prayer-meeting was being held in Parliament for the welfare of the Queen and the Royal Family.

were signs that the popularity of the Monarchy, as measured by the MORI polls (*Sunday Times*, 13 December 1992), had declined considerably.

Tony Benn MP, the republican old-timer, suddenly discovered *four* separate groups of republican opinion in 1992, instead of the usual *one* who simply believed that the Monarchy was "fundamentally undemocratic".* The new trio, he said, consisted of first, a group backed by the City favouring European federation, who would find a nationalist monarchy "a big obstacle"; second, a group of republican newspaper proprietors who had discovered there was more money in attacking the Royal Family than in glorifying it; and third, there was "the public", which, he said, "has realised it must pay for the Royal Family out of its own pocket through taxes". The Queen has neatly punctured this last group by her announcement about paying income tax; and frankly, I cannot see the other three groups whipping up a genuine republican movement, with close-run votes in Parliament and demos in Trafalgar Square.

Hugh Massingberd, editor of *Burke's Guide to the British Monarchy* (1977), described modern republicans as "a fairly unimaginative crew". However, at least one reader has found the language in Tom Nairn's republican volume, *The Enchanted Glass: Britain and its Monarchy* (1988), rather too imaginative for comfort. Speaking of the Sovereign he writes: "a nationalist emotivity informs the concrete emotivity of the Sovereign". Does this mean that a glimpse of the Sovereign makes us want to serve "Queen and Country"? If so, we monarchists quite agree. We have

The Monarchy, London Weekend Television, August 1992.

always known that the Queen generates patriotism.

A variety of republican opinions found their way into print in 1992, but not of a kind to get a real fire-ball rolling. Some were expressed by Jacobites, who merely rejected the special case of Queen Elizabeth II's Hanoverian descent. Again, in a democratic age an hereditary monarchy was thought to be at a certain disadvantage. On the other hand, if we are religious, we have the advantage of leaving the choice of monarch to "Provvy" — as Jeremy Bentham, the eighteenth-century rationalist, used to call Providence. Other old-timers had some more conventional arguments against the Monarchy, which they saw as buttressing the nation's weaknesses, encouraging the people to cling to their past and "wallow in dreams". But arguments which failed to convince in the 1970s are not likely to work in an even less creative period. Finally, there is a good old partisan argument: the Monarchy is Conservative. One might add that while the Church of England used to be called the Conservative Party at prayer, the Royal Family has become the Conservative Party at the opera (soap). However, though soap opera does have something to do with criticisms of the modern Monarchy, it has nothing to do with political parties.

Few of today's anti-monarchists seem to have the fire in the belly that blazed away in their predecessors. Take again the case of the journalist Mylius, who collaborated in writing a republican pamphlet, *The Liberator*, which falsely accused King George V of bigamy. At least Mylius's hatred of kingship was genuine. To him, the Monarchy was a "sickening, beastly monstrosity". How utterly different from Tony Benn, who has no animus against the Queen personally and hopes that, after being voted off the throne, she and her family will live happily ever after as "respected citizens". But will that day ever arrive? The *Guardian* on 29 June 1992 questioned Lord Massereene and Ferrard about the chances of a revolution establishing a British republic. He replied: "Revolution? I can't imagine a revolution in England. It rains too much." So we already have a "wet climate" favourable to the status quo.

Perhaps the oddest reasons for republicanism were advanced by Lady Selina Hastings and Sir Peregrine Worsthorne. Worsthorne believes that neither the Conservatives' meritocracy nor Labour's egalitarianism can find a place for a hereditary monarchy. "So what should British monarchists do? I fear the answer is embrace republicanism, not because we love the Monarchy too little but because we love it too much."* Selina Hastings thinks that we should stop running a monarchical system since we treat our Royal Family worse than animals. Her article in the *Spectator* is illustrated by a miserable Diana weeping into an upturned crown.†

A message somewhat similar to Tony Benn's is delivered by Robert Harris of the *Sunday Times*, who finds the most deadly opponents of the Monarchy in "the new right". They accuse it, not of "privilege" like the old left, but of being "inefficient", "expensive" and "unmeritocratic". Stephen Haseler heralds his own new book on *Britain: A European Republic* with an article declaring that the future constitution must be ready for implementation the minute

Sunday Telegraph, 29 November 1992.
†*Spectator*, June 1992.

the reign of Elizabeth II comes to an end. "Who wants Charles III?" I fear that sprightly journalist Janet Daley may have had the same thought when she wrote in *The Times* that we should retain the Monarchy until the end of the Queen's reign. "By then, however, we might just have found a rather more sensible way to preserve our spiritual inheritance than by embedding it in the person of a single, fallible human being."

One republican writer who likes a joke (most are deadly serious) is Philip Hall (*Royal Fortune*), who is tickled by the absurdity of pitying the Royal Family for their hard work and harder lot. If we want to relieve them of their sufferings, we should abolish them. *Private Eye*'s joke on 6 November 1992 was rather more elaborate. Reporting on the likely closure of the "House of Windsor Safari Park" through lack of public support, it suggested that the kindest move would be to put the Wales' and other creatures to sleep, since they "cannot fend for themselves and there is no demand for them elsewhere . . . but the sentimentalists would be up in arms".

However, when the republic is assumed to have arrived, the arguments do not go away. Who is to be president? Ludovic Kennedy fancies a judge or an ex-ambassador, like Sir Nicholas Henderson, an inspired choice. Quite a few stalwarts say we can do without a head of state: "Let the Prime Minister do it." Others, including the ironical Selina Hastings, suddenly discover that, after all, there is no one quite like the Queen:

It is true [writes Lady Selina] that the Queen, cold, competent and incorruptible, is superb at the job and would be lost without it, but then why not, after doing away with the Monarchy, appoint the Queen as President? Let her live in the Palace, keep the footmen, wear the robes, but, with the exception of the consort, move out the family and hangers-on.

This kind of attitude is not the stuff of which true republicans are made. The presidential argument usually ends up with a poll being taken in which the Queen comes top; or in denunciations of "seedy politicians", including Lady Thatcher, who will be put forward as presidential vote-winners. Indeed, the horror of a president is one of the sharpest weapons in the anti-republican armoury, just as the effeteness of the public under a monarchy is the chief weapon of their republican opponents. A favourite phrase has evolved to occupy an honoured place in the republican bible: In republics the people are *citizens*; under the Crown they are *subjects*.

So what of John Major's "Citizens' Charter"? We have yet to hear of a "Subjects' Charter", at least since the days of bad King John.

Frivolity apart, there seems to be no expanding movement for presidential government in Britain. This does not mean that gradual change — evolution — is not the best climate for a democratic monarchy's survival. There are several areas in which the Windsors might be advised to put their house in apple-pie order. Some of them have been dealt with in Chapter 6. The issues of royal marriages and the press remain to be considered here. One word of warning, however: it is increasingly important that the Crown should not seem to be changing under pressure, although at present this may not be possible. The classic example of that mistake occurred in 1957, when the young Queen's abolition of débutantes and other reforms appeared to be inspired by the valid criticisms of Malcolm Muggeridge and Lord Altrincham. In fact, the changes had been decided on quite a long time before, but the timing of the announcements was wrong.

Royal marriage has never been the easiest of undertakings. In the old days it could be a blind date or at least, marriage by portrait. We all know that George IV was horrified at Caroline of Brunswick's inelegance, partly due to carelessness about the use of soap and water or the wearing of clean underclothes. Not so many of us realise that Caroline was equally disappointed by George's failure to live up to his dashing portrait. He was "very fat", she said. Neither the handsome Monarch nor the lovely Princess was the same unappetising person who later turned up at the altar. The helplessness of the royal personage compared with the power of the court painter is illustrated by the fate of James II. In 1687, one year before his forced abdication as a Catholic and exile, King James's image on a silver medal was nothing if not regal, with its rippling wig, glossy laurel wreath and curling lips and nostrils. When the artist Mignard painted him in exile, he was described as "enfeebled, chimerical and foolish". In other words, he apparently lost his virility, wits and contact with reality ("chimerical") on losing his throne.

By the Victorian age, royal marriage according to Victoria herself was at best "a lottery" (as were all marriages) and at worst a "schocking [sic] alternative" to domestic servitude. Victoria made the "schocking" choice, and it turned out to be the right one. Sixteen years later her eldest daughter Vicky was facing one of the potentially "schocking" aspects of a marriage of convenience with complete equanimity. Engaged to Fritz, Crown Prince of Prussia, she admitted quite happily that the real reason for her marriage was a "useful alliance".* Today a useful political alliance would not be the hidden reason for a royal wedding. People would expect it to be a love-match though based also on well-understood compatibilities. Nevertheless, there are certain historical restrictions on British royal marriages that do nothing to encourage liberty of choice.

Two Acts of Parliament were designed in the eighteenth century to save the country from Roman Catholic or otherwise unsuitable royalties. Since the exile of King James II there has never been another Catholic monarch or consort. When Prince Michael of Kent married Catholic Princess Marie-Christine, he had to renounce his place in line for the throne — a sacrifice that many people might feel was well worth making.

Whatever historical justification existed for the 1701 Act of Settlement, as it was called, none will remain in the twenty-first century. It is said that Princess Astrid of Luxembourg was ruled out as a possible bride for Prince Charles on the grounds of the Act of Settlement, as robustly expounded by Norman Tebbit and other Parliamentarians. "It would signal the end of the British Monarchy", said Tebbit "by bringing it under the reach of Rome". Such views are out of touch with the Europe of the future. In

---

*As the alliance and match brought forth the Kaiser, usefulness to the world and Britain might be doubted.

addition, the restrictions of the act have particular relevance to the present separation of the Prince and Princess of Wales. There is an ironic truth in Prince Charles's words spoken on television in 1969, twelve years before his marriage: "When you marry in my position you . . . have to choose somebody very carefully, I think, who could fill the particular role . . . The one advantage of marrying a princess, for instance, or somebody from a royal family is that they do know what happens."

The second Act of Parliament that needs repealing in the interests of personal freedom and human rights is the one originally intended to give King George III control over his sons' marriages. It is high time that the Royal Marriages Act of 1772 was repealed. Last invoked when Princess Margaret wished to marry Group Captain Peter Townsend, a young victim of a wartime failed marriage, it enabled the British Cabinet virtually to prevent the marriage because Townsend had been divorced. Less than forty years later the divorced Princess Anne was happily marrying Commander Tim Laurence in Crathie Church. Laws governing the Monarchy do change, but not quickly enough.

At the risk of irritating the reader by constantly lauding the Danish royal system, I must point out that the Protestant (Lutheran) Church of Denmark does permit divorce, though remarriage must take place in the national church. It seems essential that this country should use its breathing-space (the Prince and Princess at present are officially said to have no plans for divorce) to work out a three-point plan for the future, by which the heir to the throne should be free to divorce, to remarry and to remarry in church. He would only be doing what his sister has done, and though his position as future Head of the Church is special, "the Sabbath", along with the Church, "is made for man, not man for the Sabbath".

None of these suggestions for change, whether in taxation, style of Court, deference, honours, accessibility or royal marriage could be carried through without a change in the media's sense of responsibility. The press must be truly self-regulating. That it is capable of being so is shown by its behaviour over "Dianagate" and "Camillagate" from 1989 to 1992; though unhappily its self-denial did not last. It is no use the rest of us trying to appeal to the tabloids through violent censure or moderate sympathy. They must make the change themselves. One of the Queen's former private secretaries, Michael Shea, contributed three articles to *The Times* in which he admitted that the tabloids had a redeeming feature: they were sometimes "funny". The result of his plea for moderation was nil. Judging by their contemptuous response, Shea might just as well have abused them throughout. The tabloids were not interested in praise or blame, only in one thing — sales. Is it possible to limit the intrusive nastiness without interfering with the legitimate freedom of the press?

Two disreputable tools of their trade should be vetoed. A law of trespass could prevent misuse of the 500-mm lens, though one would hope a warning to the Royal Family not to stand too near to the boundaries of their properties could be avoided.

Again, the publication of personal conversation obtained by the tapping of private telephones should clearly have been made illegal, thus preventing the "Dianagate" and "Camillagate" tapes. Proper punishment could have left behind some extremely crestfallen editors and a retired bank manager eager to go into even deeper retirement.

How far should the Royal Family themselves resort to the courts directly in hitting back at intrusion by the press? It is true that the Queen did obtain an injunction and £4,000 (given to charity) from the *Sun* when they bought Stephen Barry's "memoir" of life below stairs at the Palace, but this case was uniquely straightforward and self-contained. Barry was a storeman who had signed a promise *not* to do just what he had done — break the confidential terms of his employment. And was Barry speaking the truth, for instance, when he recounted how one night a bare-footed Diana had padded down to his Palace basement and ministered to him with buttered toast? Barry was dismissed. (He later died of AIDS.) The whole affair was pathetic and outrageous.

The trouble about most cases of tabloid misbehaviour is that they are not encapsulated in one simple story, as in the Barry affair or the historic case when Prince Albert successfully sued for the theft of sketches by himself and the Queen. Another very recent example of a suitable case to act upon occurred when the *Sun* published the Queen's Christmas message two days before its delivery, the text having been given them, according to the newspaper, by a BBC employee.* But taking a long, complex case to court could leave the Royal Family worse off than they were before. As Prince Michael pointed out, it could benefit no

---

*The Queen, in fact, sued the *Sun*, who apologised and offered to pay £200,000 to Save the Children Fund. She accepted.

one but the tabloids. All sorts of side issues could be made to arise and argument to develop so that the case could run for months, to the tabloids' infinite delight.

Then what about a new law against intrusion? A suggestion of anything like press censorship immediately causes the loyal monarchists among the press tycoons to change sides and defend their erring brethren. Andrew Knight, Chairman of News International and, like his boss Rupert Murdoch, a self-proclaimed monarchist, is a case in point.* "You cannot keep the window half open," he says, defending the freedom of the press. However, there are some windows whose opening depends on public good taste, not on legal restraints.

The Press Complaints Commission (PCC) was set up in 1991 to replace the old Press Council, and was intended to be a "new watchdog" with a "last chance" to make press self-regulation work. The PCC submitted a report, issued in October 1992, to Sir David Calcutt, who in turn was expected to report in mid-January 1993 on the prospects for self-regulation. Calcutt was thought, by the new year, to favour some degree of statutory press control, operated through a tribunal and heavy fines. The immediate cross-party reaction to this (leaked) news was mixed, though most editors were predictably hostile. A defiant Kelvin MacKenzie, editor of the *Sun*, said: "I am not going to have some clapped-out judge and two busybodies [Chairman and members of the proposed tribunal] deciding what our readers want to read."

*One must take his word for his monarchism, as given in a *Spectator* article, though some monarchists (not this one among them) found the article defending the serialisation of the Morton book hypocritical.

Meanwhile, the PCC had argued that self-regulation was now working. This, it implied, was thanks to the press's "Code of Practice", especially its passage on "Privacy": "Intrusions . . . can only be justified when in the public interest." The editors of the *Sun*, the *Daily* and *Sunday Mirror, Today*, the *Sunday Times, The Times*, the *Portsmouth News, Liverpool Echo, Scotland on Sunday* and the *People* are all quoted as favourable to self-regulation and convinced of its effectiveness. Paul Dacre of the *Daily Mail* pointed out that "one man's privacy is another man's public interest", while Bill Haggerty of the *People* added that "in a free society, even the press has the right to be wrong".

At the same time, in view of the existing privacy law in France,* combined with an understandable public belief in the need to protect the privacy of all citizens, not only the Royal Family, the idea of statutory press control began to gain ground. It was impossible not to sympathise with those who urgently wished to see an end to the tabloids' "dabbling in the stuff of other people's souls". That lambent phrase owed its birth to the strong feelings of Lord McGregor of Durris, Chairman of the PCC. He had originally understood that the worst invasion of privacy in the serialisation of *Diana: Her True Story* (the account of attempted suicides by the young mother of two schoolboys — "Offensive") was due to the intrusive press.

Suddenly, in the second week of January 1993, the two

*Although the impact of the French privacy law must not be exaggerated (its fines are nearly always very low), it does often achieve one of its purposes: it is obeyed, so raising the standard of good taste. In Germany the freedom of the press is protected by being written into the constitution.

areas of newspaper interest — the press itself and the "royals" — merged into one red-hot, lava-like stream. Lord McGregor had, in fact, no use for curbs on the press to protect the Royal Family, since he had made a devastating discovery while chairing his commission. Princess Diana had "invaded her own privacy" by trying to "manipulate" certain national newspapers into telling the story of her marriage difficulties from her personal angle. Not surprisingly, McGregor felt acute "embarrassment". The "stuff of other people's souls" had been deliberately set out for inspection.

As for Calcutt, it looked as if only the attacks in his report on electronic snooping would be implemented. There would be no tribunal and no heavy fines. The chaotic nature of events should also be noted. So numerous were the leaks (for instance, a private letter from McGregor to Calcutt leaked to the *Guardian*) that publication of the Calcutt Report had to be brought forward. Otherwise it would have been one long *déjà vu*. On Tuesday 12 January, the *Mirror*'s headline referred to "Charles, Di and the Dirty Tricks", as though the Princess's communications with the tabloids were on a par with the notorious "dirty tricks" of the media. Not only that, but McGregor had specifically exempted Prince Charles from the charge of "recruiting the tabloids" in his own interests, yet the tabloids ran it as a proven part of their story.

On the very next day, the other lava stream began to flow. Two months after the *Mirror* announced the existence of the "Camillagate" tape, the news broke of the actual tape's publication in Australia — by *New Idea* magazine, forty-five per cent owned by Rupert Murdoch. The *Sun* immediately jumped to the worst conclusion: "Six minute love tape could cost Charles throne." By the end of that week people all over the world had read faxes of the tape. The worst to be said of it was that it showed "immaturity"; the best, that it was "touching" and had a "gift for earthy language" — and anyway, it had been made over three years earlier so that all passion might now be spent. There are said to be twenty-seven more tapes.

Who made the tape? That was the next question. One school of thought suggested that it had been stolen from MI5, who had bugged the Prince for his own good — in other words to protect him from the IRA! The fact that it was stolen from *someone*, again strengthened the case for Calcutt.

How did the press emerge from this extraordinary scenario? The best gloss that can be put on the whole affair from the media's point of view is a negative one: at least the press sat on the tape for three years, as already mentioned, and, but for the new idea of *New Idea*, might be sitting on it still.

And how has it affected the Prince of Wales's future? Are the indignant readers of the *Sun* correct in predicting that "sly Di" (no longer "shy") is "to blame for ruining Charles's chances of being King"? They should take heart from four significant statements, all made on Black Friday, 13 January, and quoted in the *Daily Mail*.

Ned Sherrin, the radio presenter, said: "I hope this won't affect the Monarchy. It would not even call for comment if it was anyone other than Charles and Camilla." Norman Stone, Professor of History at Oxford, thought that "it would be insanity to ask someone to abdicate over a thing like this". Matthew Evans, managing director of Faber and Faber, publishers, did not believe that Charles should relinquish the throne; "after all, if people were disqualified from very high office for adultery, we'd have no one left to run the country". And Sebastian Faulks of the *Guardian* said that Charles should see it through and refuse "to be beaten by the buggers and their telephoto lenses".

Lastly, what advice did the Prince of Wales decide to take? His intentions, at least as reported in the Sunday broadsheets, were as beguilingly contradictory as one would expect such reports to be. According to the *Sunday Telegraph*, on 17 January, he intended to be King, and to this end was ready to "accept a celibate way of life to win back the public confidence he believes is vital to guarantee succession to the throne". But suppose we turn to the *Observer* of the same date: "Prince sees Queen at Sandringham as succession doubts mount. Charles: 'I don't want to be King.'" (A week later, however, the *Observer* apologised for attributing this statement to Prince Charles.)

It is, in fact, clear from the whole tenor of the Prince's life that he intends to succeed.

Due to the inventions of modern science — long lenses and mobile telephones — an updating in the control of electronic surveillance is now required. Together with proposed improvement in media attitudes, including more understanding and gentleness towards the Royal Family, we should now have a multi-faceted and visible programme for changes in many aspects of royal life. The last question must therefore be this: what are the characteristics of the two royal figures who would be most involved in handling the updated Monarchy? It is primarily through the Queen and Prince

Charles personally that it must be made to work. Though in case of a fatal accident to the Prince of Wales there is a successor available in the person of his elder son, to carry on the work.

The young Prince, born in 1982, would require a regent if he succeeded as King William V while still under the age of eighteen, the natural regent being his elder uncle, Prince Andrew, Duke of York. To find another case of a possible regency, we have to go right back to the reign of King William IV. His heir, Princess Victoria, was to celebrate her eighteenth birthday on 24 May 1837. Her uncle, the King, virtually on his death-bed well before that auspicious date, survived until 20 June by sheer will-power, it seemed, thus ensuring that Victoria's mother, the Duchess of Kent, should not achieve the regency she was thought to crave. Such were the animosities that weakened the Monarchy of those days.

The Prince of Wales is in many ways ideally suited to the situation that would face him. Maybe some of the tabloids would give him a less than steady back-up, but we need not worry over much about that. Their views are volatile. This fact is well illustrated by two towering headlines written within a month of each other: "I WON'T BE KING", sobs Charles in the *News of the World* on 15 November; "I WILL BE KING", promises Charles in the *Sun* on 12 December.

It has long been evident that the Prince of Wales intends to be King. His personal preparations for kingship are becoming ever more energetic and varied, his wish being to explore and understand every aspect of the nation's life. He has reached certain conclusions which can be extracted from studying his Trusts and other projects. The first is that communities can achieve results that are far beyond the reach of individuals working separately. "Together we work" is the motto designed to pinpoint the ideals of "Business in the Community". The Prince himself invites business leaders to visit local communities in his company, so that he personally is part of the "we" who are working together. I saw the same principle illustrated during a large meeting followed by seminars held in Pentonville Prison to report on the work of the Prince for helping young offenders. His manner of speaking is relaxed and he usually begins with the kind of personal joke that you will not find in a printed joke-book. At Pentonville the Prince referred to the hardness of the chairs that had been brought from the chapel for him and all of us — as hard, he might have added, as the hard labour that happily no longer exists. The recent foundation of his new Institute of Architecture shows that his aim was never merely to call modern architecture rude names — "stump", "carbuncle" — but to encourage students who have positive ideas. He hopes to reintroduce them to, among other things, "the delicate thread of wisdom that connects us with the work of our forebears". He adds:

> I should perhaps stress that the aim of the Institute's teaching will be to produce practitioners, not just theoreticians; practitioners who, rooted in traditions, are well aware of the new materials, technologies, and ways of building offered by our own times.

It is necessary to add something about "the job specification" of a Prince of Wales. The important point is that such a thing does not exist. He has to invent it. People argue that he should "do one big thing properly, rather than keep so many balls in the air". Such a policy would be a great deal simpler for him, but it has one serious drawback: it would prevent the future King from meeting thousands of people that he can now meet. It would keep him from learning about a wide range of things that go on in the country. Incidentally, when somebody explains, "The trouble with him is that he hasn't got a job, that's what's wrong with him," it usually means that they have disagreed with something he has just said.

The next key word after "job" is "frustrated". Why do so many chroniclers of the Royal Family believe that they are frustrated? The reason is not because they *are*, but because they sometimes *say* they are. An honest student of human nature who knows the royal clan well argues that they often talk about their frustration from an unconscious fear that otherwise people will think their lives are too easy. Be that as it may, the Prince did once complain about his frustrating job — and has never been allowed to forget it. When a Qantas air hostess condoled with him on his "rotten, boring job", he commented, on relating the story to his friends, that sadly it was true. However, that incident occurred when he was still in his twenties, whereas he is now forty-four. If he is still occasionally frustrated, it is only when people keep saying he is frustrated.

No one could really be frustrated who believes so passionately in dialogue. Working together through dialogue, that is the Prince's practical philosophy in a nutshell.

Despite his admirable beliefs, he is said to be impatient with his co-workers and unable to keep his staff. The impatience may well be a weakness, since it is often found in practical intellectuals who hope to turn theory into reality.

Cecil Rhodes, once the uncrowned king of Southern Africa, lamented on his death-bed: "So little done; so much to do." As for the legend about the Prince's staff, it is based on two particular facts both of which have been misinterpreted. First, the appointment of Christopher Airey as the Prince's private secretary. Airey's departure after one year caused a furore in the press, even though it was mutually agreed that the appointment had been a mistake. Second, there is an arrangement in the Prince's office by which certain secretaries are seconded to it for periods of two years. This system gives the mistaken impression of an unflatteringly rapid turnover.

In fact, the Prince of Wales's intellect and achievements are all enviable. Not since Prince George, later George IV, has the nation been able to look forward to a future monarch with such artistic gifts. The nation should show its appreciation of its present good fortune.

Prince Charles has tried to handle his own periods of emotional stress and strain with a régime of physical exercise, preferably something challenging like polo. Without vigorous exercise he says he would go "potty". He recognises the need for balance between the claims of the State and of the Royal Family as individuals. He has a "Vision for Britain", and in the book of that title he cites such desirable changes as the creation of "a new sense of belonging and a sense of order". "I believe that when a man loses contact with the past he loses his soul." If some of these enthusiasms seem to show a touch of eccentricity, this is always the way with the thoughts of innovators — until their experiments are accepted and become part of orthodoxy. This is the time for Prince Charles to harness his allegedly eccentric beliefs to the service of his country. When he is King most of that will have to stop. "Uneasy lies the head that wears a crown" — particularly if that head, like King James I's, is perpetually chasing after new theories.

But will our future Charles III ever wear the crown? Plenty of alternative suggestions have been aired. For example, that we should have Queen Anne II instead of King Charles III; or that William V should succeed immediately to his grandmother with Prince Andrew, if necessary, as regent.

The separated Princess of Wales is convinced, we are told, that neither she nor Prince Charles will ever succeed; this being a "gut reaction". Princess Diana's gut reactions have been and must be taken seriously, especially insofar as they affect Prince William. Apparently, she intends to bring him up to believe that he, rather than his father, will be the next King. Were she to pursue this line of thought — and let us hope she does not intend to do so — this could produce difficulties in the father/son relationship.

Are there any reasons why the Prince of Wales himself should decide not to ascend the throne? I only know of one, which he touched on in September 1992, three months before the separation. If Parliament, through swingeing taxation or some other form of financial pressure, deprived him of personal independence, he would go. He said:

I think it of absolute importance that the Monarch should have a degree of financial independence from the State. I am not prepared to take on the position of sovereign of this country on any other basis. I must have independence, and you can only have that through financial independence. If it [royal taxation] is reorganised it must be done in such a way that there is no danger of being in the pocket of the State. . . . It would all have to be very carefully arranged.

Taxation of ninety-seven per cent (a figure that the Prince named as unacceptable) would probably signify the arrival of an extreme left-wing revolution. By which time the Monarchy would already have been abolished, along with many other institutions such as the free press, the independent judiciary, the established church and the House of Lords. This will not happen unless in the next quarter-century Great Britain has become derelict, with the "Great" in its title a laughable absurdity.

"Moderation in all things." That is the motto on which Elizabeth II pinned her hopes in the film celebrating the fortieth anniversary of her accession. It is a motto that sounds as old as civilisation (it came from ancient Greece in half the number of words that we need today — *meden agan* — and is still as fresh as a thought generated for a coming new century). If we want to know what the Queen, on whom so much depends, is really like, we should just say those four words: "Moderation in all things"; or, in their original form, translated: "Nothing too much".

What are the virtues fostered in a queen who stands for moderation? First of all, an admiration for order. Not order in the sense of a medal, nor order in the sense of a command, but order in the sense of system, regularity, neatness, tidiness. When the writer A. N. Wilson watched on television the burning of Windsor Castle, he remembered that it had been Princess Elizabeth's childhood home, so he turned to Crawfie's "Memoirs" of that childhood. He found that *The Little Princesses*, despite its cloying vulgarity, gave more insights into the Queen's true character than any details in Morton about Diana. Wilson sums her up as "the stoical, strange little heroine", the strangeness being due to the child's preoccupation with order. Sometimes she would get out of bed at night to make sure that her clothes were all neatly folded on her chair and her shoes in perfect order underneath. At this stage her attention to orderliness was clearly obsessive. Who knows but that this early exaggeration later caused her to appreciate moderation.

Another ingredient of moderation is calm — the very opposite to hysteria or any illness described as "nervosa". The Queen is notably calm. When the intruder Michael Fagan invaded her bedroom, she not only remained calm herself but kept him calm also, together with a pack of excitable corgis. She can cope. After *annus horribilis* had worked up to a crescendo with the fire of Windsor and the Wales's separation, she appeared calm and smiling at Princess Anne's wedding.

A royal philosophy of moderation demands no hasty decisions. If anything, you must move a little slower than the pace of events; never in advance. You must also try to avoid answering back, for that automatically raises the temperature and prolongs the clash. The Queen was clearly behind her eldest son when he refused to take part in the first skirmishes preliminary to his matrimonial separation, though urged to retaliate by friends and foes alike.

The Queen is not deflected in her life by sideshows. She goes for what matters, the essentials. Take clothes. In her position, the main point over the years is to be recognised. Fashion is irrelevant, even dangerous. She does not want the crowds to inspect two identically fashionably dressed figures and wonder which one is the Queen. Anyone who visited the "Sovereign" exhibition at the Victoria & Albert Museum in 1992, marking the Queen's fortieth anniversary, must have been struck by one fact: all the Queen's coats and dresses that were exhibited, whatever the date, obviously came out of the same wardrobe: the same cut, the same collars, the same kind of colours. They were unquestionably the Queen's. That was what mattered.

Moderation rules out extravagance. The Queen is sensitive to her people's feelings and on at least two important occasions she has vetoed eye-catching display. First, at her Silver Wedding in 1972 when the country was under economic strain; second, at her "Ruby Jubilee" in 1992, when the recession was in full downward swing. Looking back on 1992 people will be able to remember only the wrong kind of fireworks: no magnificent displays in Hyde Park but flames in Windsor Castle and rockets in the Royal Family.

Moderation in party political views has a special meaning for the Queen, which she well understands. However moderate, such views must not exist as far as she is concerned. Neutrality not moderation is required of her in party politics. Fortunately for the country, she learnt it once and for all at her father's knee.

With moderation goes modesty, an unexpected royal modesty that her people find irresistible. The fortieth anniversary film gave us new glimpses into this trait. We have already seen the Queen confessing that her diary was "quite small. I can't write any other way." When she came to touch on the subject of gardening, the same modesty was apparent. Yes, she loved it, "It does soothe . . .", but, "I'm only a weeder really." The story comes to mind of a friend lunching with the Queen Mother at Frogmore and arriving to find the Queen in the garden, putting in a few minutes' weeding for her mother. *They also serve who only kneel and weed.*

One final thought: is it indeed to be "moderation in *all* things"? In love, for instance? There is an equally powerful saying that can be put up against the claims for moderation: "You can't have too much of a good thing." There has been an insidious suggestion going around to the effect that both the Queen and the Prince of Wales are cold, preoccupied, lacking in love. The Princess of Wales is seen to advantage in her lauding of love: from practical demonstrations by jumping into her two small sons' beds to cuddle them, to a speech in which she recommended the prevention of drug abuse in adolescence by hugging in childhood. "There is a hugger", she said, "in every household."

Princess Diana has not publicly accused her mother-in-law of coldness, but Sarah, Duchess of York, has done so. She was reported as complaining that on many mountain walks at Balmoral with the Queen, she had tried in vain to discuss her relations with Prince Andrew. Up and down they trudged, talking pleasantly of everything on earth — scenery, horses, the ubiquitous dogs — but never a personal word. Clearly the Queen chose to wait for a discussion about her son until he himself was present to attend the meeting, which duly took place. Meanwhile, the Queen had been misunderstood.

There is no coldness but a great deal of reserve. The Queen

is sensitive and reticent. The royal job could not have been performed so magnificently for forty years without a certain degree of remoteness. Queen Margrethe of Denmark has explained that situation in her own memoirs: the remoteness of a monarch is not a question of temperament but of doing the job properly. Far from being inaccessible by nature, Queen Margrethe nevertheless finds that there are times when a monarch must keep her distance. Today the fashion is for the media to drag or entice every heart on to the sleeve. But rather than wear her heart on her sleeve, Queen Elizabeth II would give the impression of not having one. Yet anyone who knows her never doubts her warmth of heart.

It is sometimes said that the Queen's reserve caused shyness in Prince Charles. That is not the case. They both inherited the private side of their personality from the same source: King George VI. But whereas the King most happily chose the outgoing Queen Elizabeth, now the Queen Mother, as his complement and mediator, while the Queen was equally successful in choosing Prince Philip, Princess Diana, though outgoing, was not able to work her magic on Prince Charles.

The magic was there all right, perhaps in too much evidence for her own good. Her public took pleasure in building up her gifts into quasi-supernatural powers, so that some people began to feel they were at Lourdes, or some such healing shrine. Queen Victoria maintained a better perspective on this kind of royal magic. She wrote after visiting a hospital during the Crimean War: "It is very gratifying to feel that what one can do so easily, gives so much pleasure."

The Princess of Wales's magic is nothing to do with royal

mystique. It is a personal projection and would remain with her even if the Prince and she were divorced. Though less and less encouraged in today's climate, the famous "mystique" of monarchy nevertheless envelops the Queen herself — but not necessarily all her family, who would not want it — in an unmistakable aura. To republicans, its contemplation weakens our brains ("Give us this day our daily trance"); to the rest of us its presence increases our understanding — understanding of what we mean by the nation, its past and future.

We saw the mystique in the Queen's film, *Elizabeth R*: palaces, castles, pipers, a Highland reel with the royal dancers in swirling kilts and brilliant white skirts like cumulus clouds — the Princess Royal and Commander Tim Laurence together. At the same time the Queen was careful to show us the non-mystical side of her experience: the passion for pedigrees and breeding whether in racehorses, cattle or dogs. To her, this creative excitement would make arable farming devoid of animals seem "boring". The fact that her own pedigree goes back so far, despite deviations, gives her a natural interest in continuity and tradition. But you can keep tradition going only if you are adaptable and responsive. Of this the Queen is well aware. She is no Bourbon, the royal house that learnt nothing and forgot nothing. "Let them eat cake," said Marie Antoinette when she heard that the people were desperate for bread. Queen Elizabeth II, in such a situation, would limit the Palace to ration cards and coupons, as did her parents during the war, arrange for emergency bread deliveries and throw in meals-on-wheels.

"The Monarchy has the magic of survival"; so said the distinguished writer Anthony Sampson. It is still surviving many years later. Will it go on?

That somewhat mysterious phrase "magic of survival" offers one clue. Survival depends on some form of "magic" still adhering to it, like the bloom on a plum. If the bloom entirely disappears and with it the fruit's beauty, that particular food may not in future be chosen above other rival nutrients. Subject to necessary changes already outlined here, the Monarchy will keep its bloom, as well as being good for us. The bloom of romance, myth, magic — call it what you like — will continue to give the Monarchy survival power for as long as it is safe to guess.

This is exemplified by the fact that one person out of three in this country has dreamt about the Queen. In other words, she has got into our subconscious, a very strategic place to be. In questioning a thousand people, Brian Masters (*Dreams of H.M. the Queen and Other Members of the Royal Family*) found that Elizabeth and Philip were always pleasant, parental figures even when the dreamers were republicans. Frequently they took tea with the Queen or gave her assistance. One dreamer, who was rescuing her from being run away with by Philip's polo ponies, noticed that she was wearing wellies under her gorgeous gown. Another dreamer helped the adored Queen Mother when she had lost her passport at Heathrow airport and was surrounded by twenty hectic corgis. "I am sorry, Ma'am," said the dreamer "but you will have to stay in quarantine with the dogs. We can fix up a perfectly comfortable kennel for you for six months." Yet another dreamer was surprised to meet the Queen under Niagara Falls. "'You see, dear,'

HM said, 'we've got this State Visit to do and one always has to look at the Falls, and say nice things about them.' There she stood, gallons of water showering upon her, waving and smiling in a mac and crown." I cannot resist adding my own small dream contribution. I was at a charity garden party and Her Majesty, our patron, was inside one of the tents. Outside, between two tents, was a green garden chair on which was tidily piled a set of most exquisite satin and lace lingerie. I realised with no surprise that it belonged to our patron because of its charm and neatness.

Emerging from dreamland, it is necessary to return to the positive things that the Monarchy gives to this country. It will stand or fall by them. There is no need to scratch around and produce the money brought in by tourists. Britannia would have come to a pretty pass if tourists were to be the arbiters of her constitution.

It *might* survive because it moves with the times. Emerald Cunard, the famous socialite, once tried to flatter Edward VIII with the spurious claim, "You are the modernist [sic] man in England", to which Edward replied with rare good sense, "Oh no, I only want to move with the times."

It *might* survive because it is above class and party. During the miners' strike of the 1970s, the miners' wives, including Mrs Scargill, appealed to the Queen to put their case to the relevant ministers. And in 1992 the miners themselves, when on a visit to Strasbourg about pit closures, revealed afterwards that they got a much warmer welcome from Prince Charles, whom they ran into, than from the MEPs.

It *might* survive because it unites the people; whereas the election of a president, if fiercely fought, could earmark and emphasise their divisions.

It *will* survive because the people want it. They may not know why, but they know they do. They want it to work well. They will endure some bad years, such as the Abdication year and *annus horribilis*, in order that the good years may return. We can put explanatory words into their mouths if we like. The people want the Queen to remind them of their history, both glorious and grievous; they want her to be admired as their Queen and to speak for them with pride in Europe and the Commonwealth; to tell the world not to believe that they are flaked out; to allow them to believe, deep down, that someone is caring about them, in reality and also certainly and unquestionably as in a dream. Above all, they want a Head of State who is neutral because she has never belonged to a political party; a fit guardian of the constitution because she has no personal ambition, only the wish to serve. If that turns out to be still a fair description of the Monarchy in the twenty-first century, any exchange would be robbery.

It will survive as the fittest system for this country. It will survive because its existence keeps out other objectionable systems. It will survive because its destruction would bring down with it many other things that we do not want to lose. It will survive because it is no longer dependent on the aristocracy or an unreformed House of Lords. It will survive because it is equally above all social groups, whether the upper classes, the middle classes or the poor; and does not promote the interests of one class at the expense of another. It will survive because we have fashioned it over the centuries to our taste, and it is capable of going through that process of refashioning as often as we wish, or as our imagination dictates. It is a splendid thing, and our own.

EPILOGUE

On 11 February 1993, the Prime Minister again announced in Parliament that Her Majesty and the Prince of Wales had volunteered to pay income tax as from 6 April. "Pay as you reign", said the *Sun* brightly. The Royal Family's popular and principled initiative was welcomed by all the political parties though not by all individual MPs. Tony Benn called the tone of Parliament's welcome "creepy-crawly", whereas others called it "muted", perhaps because it would have been inappropriate to shout for joy at the Queen's sacrifice. The *Guardian* photographed the notice-board in the forecourt of Buckingham Palace giving the time of the "Next Changing of the Guard" — but on that February day the notice said "CANCELLED", seeming to symbolise the possible cancellation of certain royal rituals under the new dispensation. Another reason for the muted applause may have been that there was little in the announcement that was new. However, three points were clarified. First, negotiations had been initiated as early as February 1992 by the Queen; therefore it was the recession, not the young royals' antics, which had caused people to look askance at the Queen's (exaggerated) wealth. Second, the Queen would pay capital gains tax. Third, she would pay inheritance tax, except on bequests to her successor. Otherwise her assets would be "salami-sliced away" (Mr Major's phrase).

The discussion of the Queen's inheritance tax, and her qualified exemption from it, raised a further question. Should other aspects of the Royal Prerogative, besides the right to a tax-free status, be now reformed? For instance, it is the Sovereign's right to dissolve Parliament and to appoint the new Prime Minister. Ought this to continue unchanged?

True, the Queen's right to appoint the Prime Minister in the case of a "hung" Parliament is generally agreed to be a "grey" area; as is her right to refuse a dissolution, say, a mere six weeks after an election. But except for these "grey" areas, which may one day need to be elucidated, and where the Queen still has a certain freedom of choice, the Royal Prerogative is clear-cut and cut-and-dried. The Queen will always send for the leader of the party that can command a majority in the House of Commons. Unlike the tax situation, there is no general call for change here.

And what did Her Majesty think of it all? On the same day as the details of her historic decision were explained, she was photographed entering a community centre with a radiant smile — very different from the wan half-smile she had raised in the Guildhall three months before. Her present cheerfulness said two things: it was right to treat her as one of us; it was sensible to recognise her special position as hereditary Monarch. As for her previous tax-free condition, nothing became her like the leaving of it.

15 February 1993

INDEX

Abdication (1936), xvi, 1, 16-17;
  see also Edward VIII, King
Adeane, Sir Michael (*later*
  Baron), xxiv, 97
Adelaide, Queen of William IV,
  6, 123
Airey, Christopher, 169
Albert, Prince Consort: pays
  income tax, 26, 41;
  character, 47;
  collects art, 85;
  death, 86;
  modernising, 98;
  conservative disapproval of
    reforms, 109;
  sues for theft, 160
Albert Victor, Prince, Duke of
  Clarence ("Eddy"; Edward
  VII's son), 12
Alexandra, Queen of Edward VII,
  xv, xxvi, 10
Alexandra, Princess, 43, 74, 118,
  143
Alfred, Prince, Duke of Coburg
  (Queen Victoria's son), xv
Alice, Princess, Grand Duchess
  of Hesse (Queen Victoria's
  daughter), xiv
Alice, Princess *see* Gloucester,
  Duchess of,
Allen, Sir Douglas, 34
Altrincham, 2nd Baron *see* Grigg,
  John,

Anna of Cleves, Queen of Henry
  VIII, 8
Anne, Queen, xv, 3
Anne Boleyn, Queen of Henry
  VIII, xv, 8
Anne, Princess Royal: divorce,
  7, 103;
  Civil List allowance, 36;
  work for children, 50;
  on royal status, 82;
  and Diana on 1992 Armistice
    Day, 91;
  first wedding, 99;
  relations with father, 100-1;
  public esteem, 101-2;
  second marriage (to Tim
    Laurence), 103, 138, 148,
    158, 172, 176;
  riding, 107;
  in *Grand Knock-Out
    Tournament*, 111n;
  Queen pays allowance to, 142;
  as prospective Queen, 170
Anson, Charles, 70, 79, 125,
  129
Antrim, Louisa, Countess of,
  xxiii
Argyll, John Douglas Sutherland
  Campbell, 9th Duke of, xvi
Argyll, Duchess of *see* Louise,
  Princess
Aronson, Theo: *Monarchy in
  Transition*, 39

Arthur, Prince (Henry VIII's brother), 8

Arthur, Prince, Duke of Connaught (Queen Victoria's son), xiv, 95, 97

Astrid, Princess of Luxembourg, 157

Athelstan, King of the English, 3

Aylesford scandal (1876), 10

Aylesford, Edith, Countess of, 10

Baccarat case (1891), 10

Bagehot, Walter, xii-xiv, 75

Baker, James, xix

Baldwin, Stanley, 1

Barrantes, Susan, 52

Barnett, Joel, 31-2

Barrington-Ward, Simon, Bishop of Coventry, 128

Barry, Stephen, 160

Bartholomew, Carolyn, 57

Beaton, Cecil, xxi

Beatrice, Princess of Battenberg, (Queen Victoria's daughter), xv

Beatrice, Princess of York, 53, 62, 120

Beaumont-Dark, Antony, 38

Beaverbrook, William Maxwell Aitken, 1st Baron, 15

Benn, Tony, 38, 151, 152-3, 180

Bentham, Jeremy, 152

Beresford, Lord Charles and Lady Charles, 10-11

Blake, Peter, 113

Blandford, George Charles Churchill, Marquess of (*later* 8th Duke of Marlborough), 10

Blewitt, Sir Ralph, 31n

Blom-Cooper, Sir Louis, 65

Boyd-Carpenter, John, 28, 35

Brooke, Peter, 139

Brougham, Henry Peter, 1st Baron, 26

Brown, John, xxiii, 109

Brown, Ron, 38

Bryan, John, 62-3

Burke, Edmund, xxvii

Butler, Richard Austen (*later* Baron), 52, 124

Calcutt, Sir David, 79, 161-3

Callaghan, James, (*later* Baron), 73

"Camillagate", xxvii, 65n, 114, 159-60;
    see also Parker Bowles, Camilla

Campbell, Lady Colin: *Diana, A Princess and Her Troubled Marriage*, 55

Cannadine, Professor David, 133

Caroline, Queen of George IV, 11-12, 123, 156

Casey, John, 1, 66

Catherine of Aragon, Queen of Henry VIII, 8

Chamberlain, Joseph, xi, 109

Charles I, King, xiii, 6, 12, 85, 94

Charles II, King, 6

Charles, Prince of Wales:
    speeches, xix;
    upbringing and education, 13n,
        98, 105-6;
    marriage breakdown, 19, 45,
        54-5, 104, 108, 146-7, 159;
    on royal taxes, 21, 142-5,
        180;
    relations and conversations
        with Camilla Parker Bowles,
        23, 56, 114, 163;
    concern for son, 46, 102;
    character, activities and
        interests, 47-51, 85, 168;
    speeches to Lords, 47-8;
    political and social concerns,
        48-51, 78, 86-7, 166-7;
    and mother's possible
        abdication, 55, 71-2;
    Diana complains of, 65;
    on "curious" Monarchy, 67;
    visit to Far East, 67;
    on change, 68;
    at Queen's 40th anniversary,
        71;
    supposed rift with Queen, 72;
    view of Monarchy, 74, 83;
    and moral example, 78;
    effect of divorce on, 81;
    influenced by foreign travel
        and places, 86-8, 135;
    depicted on TV, 92;
    praises Queen Mother, 95;
    relations with father, 99-100;
    public attitude to, 105-8, 111;
    sports, 106-7, 169;
    accent, 107;
    provocative remarks, 110;
    questions press coverage, 115,
        164;
    and size of royal "firm", 120;
    and Duchy of Cornwall, 128,
        146-7;
    and "Scandinavianisation" of
        Monarchy, 135;
    on marriage, 157;
    intends to succeed to throne,
        165, 170;
    and job as Prince of Wales,
        167-8;
    relations with staff, 169;
    shyness, 175;
    welcomes miners, 178
Charlotte, Queen of George III,
    xiii
Charteris, Sir Martin (*later*
    Baron), xxv, 41, 74, 122
Cheshire, Leonard, xxvii
Church of England: and divorce,
    81
Churchill, Lord Randolph, 10,
    107
Civil List: and taxation, 25, 28-
    35;
    extent of, 36, 39;
    popular attitude to, 41;
    reduction of beneficiaries, 118-
        19, 143
Clausewitz, Karl von, 110
Cleveland Row scandal, 12
Cobbold, Cameron Fromanteel
    Cobbold, 1st Baron, 31, 34
Commonwealth: representation
    in Royal Household, 126

Cornwall, Duchy of, 128, 146

Court and Household, Royal, xxiv, 123-9, 134

Crawford, Marion (Crawfie): *The Little Princesses*, 105 & n, 172

Crown Estate, 33-4, 146

Cunard, Emerald (Maud Alice), Lady, 178

Dacre, Paul, 162

Daily Express, 72

Daily Mail, 20, 54-5, 61-2, 164

Daily Mirror, 60, 62, 67, 92, 114-15, 144, 163-4

Daley, Janet, 20-1, 154

Dawson of Penn, Bertrand Edward Dawson, Viscount, 127

débutantes, xvii, 108, 155

Dempster, Nigel, 41, 119, 123

Denmark: monarchy in, 2, 119, 130, 133-4;
divorce in, 158

Devonshire, Spencer Compton Cavendish, 8th Duke of, 79

Diana, Princess of Wales: belief in healing and work for sick, 4, 48-9, 51, 92, 176;
marriage breakdown, 18-19, 45, 54-5, 104, 108, 146-7, 158, 175;
Morton on, 23;
qualities, 51;
divorce pact with Duchess of York, 54;
bulimia, 55;
supposed suicide attempts, 56-71, 162;
encourages press, 57-8, 148, 162;
belief in paranormal, 58-9;
taped conversation with Gilby ("Dianagate"), 19, 64-5, 80, 114;
failed reconciliation with Charles, 67;
at Queen's 40th anniversary, 71;
and Anne on 1992 Armistice Day, 91;
relations with Prince Philip, 93;
denies unkindness of Queen and Philip, 94;
public attitude to, 102;
and "Camillagate" tapes, 114;
platform play, 115;
in royal "firm", 120;
and prospective coronation, 148;
disbelieves succession, 170;
image of lovingness, 174

"Dianagate", 19, 64-5, 80, 114, 159-60, 164

Dickens, Charles, ix

Dilke, Sir Charles, 109

Divine Right of Kings, xv, 3

Dryden, John, 143

Dugdale, Thomas, 1

Eadred, King of the English, 2

Eadwig, King of the English, 6

Economist, The (journal), 40

Eddy, Prince *see* Albert Victor, Prince

Edgar, King of the English, 2

Edinburgh, Duke of *see* Philip, Prince

Edmund, King of the English, 5

Edmund Ironside, King of the English, 5

Education Act (1870), xii, xvi

Edward the Confessor, King of the English, 2

Edward the Elder, King of the English, 2

Edward the Martyr, King of the English, 5

Edward II, King, 5, 6

Edward III, King, xviii, 2, 6, 12

Edward IV, King, 6

Edward V, King, 5

Edward VI, King, 6

Edward VII, King (*formerly* Prince of Wales): marriage, xv;
death, xxiv;
Coronation, xxv;
and moral example, 4;
mistresses, 6;
involved in scandals, 12;
and Select Committee on Civil List, 28n;
on art, 46-7;
prodigality, 135

Edward VIII, King (*later* Duke of Windsor): abdication, xi, 1, 16-17;
boredom at garden parties, xxii;

touched in USA, 3;
and moral example, 4;
as eldest son, 13;
marriage, 13-16;
social conscience, 84;
relations with Household, 126;
on moving with times, 178

Edward, Prince (Elizabeth II's son), 82, 111, 120, 137, 143

Eleanor of Aquitaine, Queen of Henry II, 9

Elizabeth I, Queen, 2

Elizabeth II, Queen: and prophecies of end of Monarchy, x, 8, 112;
ends presentation of débutantes, xvii, 108-9, 155;
and Garter ceremony, xix;
seriousness and dedication, xx-xxi;
and Royal Archives, xxii;
1961 visit to Ghana, xxv;
on 1992 misfortunes ("*annus horribilis*"), xvi;
and moral example, 4, 76;
children's marriages, 8;
on royal divorces, 9;
and payment of income tax, 19-21, 24-7, 29-30, 34, 37, 39-42, 126, 132, 136-7, 142, 151, 180;
wealth, 20, 29, 40, 137;
as "school prefect", 21;
Morton criticises, 23;
collections, 30;
on young royals, 43;
and children's marriage

breakdowns, 52, 111, 146-7, 172;
and possible abdication, 54;
and Duchess of York's behaviour, 62;
attitude to press photographers, 63;
popularity, 66, 155;
advises Charles and Diana to mend marriage, 67;
informality, 69;
40th anniversary of accession, 71, 169-70;
supposed rift with Charles, 72;
view of Monarchy, 73, 83, 88-90;
and press, 79;
on effect of Coronation, 81;
breeds cattle, 85;
mobile life, 89-90;
relations with Diana, 93;
and horses, 107;
Queen Mary encourages, 113;
and proposed royal sabbatical year, 115-18;
and importance of family, 117;
and size of royal "firm", 119-23;
Household, 123-9;
and Europe, 128;
visits Germany, 128;
and Duchy of Lancaster, 128;
reduced deference and ceremonial, 130-3;
and honours system, 132;
and foreign royalty, 133-6;
keeps diary, 136, 173-4;
and Windsor fire, 138-9;
1992 Guildhall speech, 140-3;
Civil List payments, 143;
injunction against *Sun*, 160;
practices moderation, 171-2;
orderliness, 172;
reserve, 173-4;
and mystique, 175-6;
in dreams, 177;
and survival of Monarchy, 179
Elizabeth the Queen Mother (wife of King George VI): Beaton photographs, xxi;
and Royal Archives, xxii;
Duchess of Windsor and, 14;
Morton criticises, 23;
Civil List allowance, 36, 143;
public effort, 51;
and Diana's fall, 56;
Diana's reaction to, 65;
on effect of Coronation, 81;
character and popularity, 95, 175;
and horses, 107
Elizabeth R (TV film), xix, 89, 136, 176
English, Sir David, 61
Eugénie, Princess of York, 53, 62, 120
Evans, Matthew, 164
Evening Standard, 62, 93

Fagan, Michael, 172
Faraday Institutes, 87
Farrer, Sir Matthew, 65
Fathers, Michael, 6-7

Faulks, Sebastian, 165
Fellowes, Lady Jane (*née*
Spencer; Diana's sister), 60,
125
Fellowes, Sir Robert, 69, 80,
124
"Fergiegate", 65 & n
Financial Times, 143-4
Fleming, Peter, xxi
Ford, Sir Edward, 142n
France: privacy law, 161 & n
Frederick, Crown Prince of
Prussia (*later* Emperor of
Germany; "Fritz"), 157

Garter, Order of, xx
George III, King, xiii, 6, 33,
158
George IV, King, 11-12, 26, 75,
135, 156
George V, King: sense of role,
xiii;
presentations to, xvii;
as example, 4;
succeeds as second son, 12;
sues Mylius, 79, 152;
conservatism, 113;
changes family name, 125;
avoids ostentation, 135
George VI, King: funeral, xvii,
xx;
as example, 4;
as second son, 12;
and Duke of Windsor, 15;
accession, 16-17;
reappoints Lascelles, 16;
income-tax exemption, 25;

and size of Royal Family,
119;
and Household, 126;
and deference, 131n;
simple tastes, 135;
reserve, 175
Germany: Queen in, 128;
press freedom, 161n
Gilbey, James, 23, 64, 93
Gladstone, William Ewart, 11
Gloucester, Princess Alice,
Duchess of, 143;
Memoirs, 39n, 117
Gloucester, Prince Henry, Duke
of, 36, 119
Gloucester, Mary, Duchess of,
27
Glover, Stephen, 124
Gordon-Cumming, Sir William,
10
Gordonstoun school, 105
Grand Knock-Out Tournament
(TV programme), 111
Graves, Robert, 82
Grigg, John (*formerly* 2nd Baron
Altrincham), 21, 126-7, 140,
156;
The Monarchy Revisited, 150
Grove, Trevor (ed.): *The Queen
Observed*, 39n
Guardian, 180
Gwynn, Nell, 6

Haggerty, Bill, 162
Hahn, Kurt, 98, 105
Hailsham, Quintin McGarel
Hogg, Baron, 131

Hall, Philip: *Royal Fortune*, 29, 31n, 39, 154
Hall, Stuart, 111n
Hamilton, William, 28, 31, 34-7
Hanson & Walles: *A Guide to Political Institutions*, 39n
Harewood, George Henry Hubert Lascelles, 7th Earl of, 7
Harold, King of the English, 6
Harris, Robert, 153
Harry, Prince (son of Charles and Diana), 54, 76, 147
Haseler, Stephen: *Britain: A European Republic*, 153
Hastings, Lady Selina, 153-5
Heald, Tim, 100
Heath, Sir Edward, xix, 147
Helena, Princess (Queen Victoria's daughter), xiv
Henderson, Sir Nicholas, 154
Henry I, King, 6
Henry II, King, 9
Henry V, King, 12
Henry VI, King, 3, 5
Henry VII, King, 6
Henry VIII, King, xv, 5, 8, 12
Henry, Prince of Battenberg ("Liko"), xv
Heseltine, Sir William, 125
Hewitt, Major James, 66
Highgrove, Gloucestershire, 49-50
Hoey, Brian: *Monarchy*, 39
Holden, Anthony, 19, 104, 108, 109, 142
honours system, 132
Houghton, Douglas, 28, 32, 35

Household *see* Court and Household, Royal
Howard, Philip: *British Monarchy*, 39, 95

Independent, The, 123

James I, King, 5
James II, King, 156-7
James, Paul: *Anne: The Working Princess*, 103
Jay, Antony, 89, 132
Jenkins, Roy (*later* Baron), 28
Jobson, Robert, 72n
John, King, 5
Johnson, Paul, 12
Johnson, Samuel, xvi
Jordan, Dorothy, 6
Juan Carlos, King of Spain, 134
Junor, Penny, 60; *Charles and Diana*, 103

Keay, Douglas, 41; *Elizabeth II*, 91
Kennedy, Ludovic, 154
Kenny, Mary, 92
Kent, Prince Edward George, Duke of, 143
Kent, Prince George, Duke of, 76, 97
Kent, Princess Marina, Duchess of, 44
Kent, Prince Michael of, 76, 115, 118, 120, 157, 160
Kent, Princess Michael of (Marie-Christine), 77, 157

Kent, Victoria, Duchess of (Queen Victoria's mother), 123, 166

Keppel, Alice, xxiv, 6, 23

King's Evil (scrofula), 3

Kinnock, Neil, 38

Knight, Andrew, 61, 161

Lamb, Lady Caroline (née Ponsonby), xxiv

Lancaster, Duchy of, 25, 35, 128

Langtry, Lillie ("Jersey Lily"), 6

Lascelles, Sir Alan ("Tommy"), 16

Laurence, Commander Tim, 148, 158, 176

Leopold, Prince, Duke of Albany (Queen Victoria's son), xiv

Lloyd George, David, 24

Longford, Elizabeth: Victoria R.I., xxii, xxv

Louis VII, King of France, 9

Louise, Princess, Duchess of Argyll (Queen Victoria's daughter), xv-xvi, 95, 97

Luce, Sir Richard, 58

McGregor of Durris, Oliver Ross McGregor, Baron, 162-3

McKay, Peter, 111

MacKenzie, Kelvin, 161

Mail on Sunday, 53-4, 58

Major, John, 142, 146, 155, 180

Mann, Rt Rev. Michael, 91

Marcus, Darryl, 129

Margaret Rose, Princess: supposed deafness and dumbness, xxiii; and Peter Townsend, 7, 158; divorce, 7; Morton criticises, 23; Civil List allowance ended, 36; children, 44; on sister being Queen, 82-3; Queen Mary encourages, 113; and people's prayers, 150

Margrethe II, Queen of Denmark, 130, 133-5, 175

Marie Antoinette, Queen of France, 176

Mary, Queen of George V, xvii, 14, 113, 119, 131n

Mary, Queen of Scots, 5

Massereene and Ferrard, John Talbot Whyte-Melville Skeffington, Viscount, 153

Massingberd, Hugh, 151

Masters, Brian: Dreams of the Queen, 177

Meir, Golda, 102

Melbourne, William Lamb, 2nd Viscount, xx, 26, 129

Mellor, David, 45

Menkes, Suzy, 83

Mignard, Pierre, 156

Mirzoeff, Michael, 89

Monckton, Walter (later 1st Viscount), 15

Money magazine, 30

Moore, Sir Philip, 125

Mordaunt, Sir Charles, 9-10

Morrow, Anne: *The Queen Mother*, 39n

Morton, Andrew: *Diana: Her True Story*, xxvi, 23, 45, 54-6, 59, 93, 100, 105, 161n

Mount, Ferdinand, xiii, 85

Mountbatten, Admiral of the Fleet Louis, 1st Earl, 13n, 15, 69, 99

Mowatt, Marina (*née* Ogilvy), 43, 74

Mowatt, Paul, 43

Muggeridge, Malcolm, 156

Munster, 1st Earl of (son of William IV, by Mrs Jordan), 26

Murdoch, Rupert, 61, 161, 163

Mylius, Edward Frederick, 79, 131, 152

Nairn, Tom: *The Enchanted Glass: Britain and its Monarchy*, 39, 151

Neil, Andrew, 61

New Idea (magazine), 163

News of the World, 166

Nicolson, Sir Harold, 21

Nicolson, Nigel, 133

Norman, Edward, 148

Observer, 165

Ogilvy, Sir Angus, 43

Pannell, Charlie, 33

Parker Bowles, Andrew, 23

Parker Bowles, Camilla (*née* Shand), 23, 57, 114, 164

Peel, Sir Robert, 26, 27n, 143

Philip, Prince, Duke of Edinburgh: wildlife interests, xix-xx;
on voluntary change, 21;
Morton criticises, 24;
Civil List allowance, 36, 143;
attitude to press photographers, 63;
view of Monarchy, 74, 83;
and press, 80;
and "ordinary blokes", 83;
travels, 89-90;
relations with Diana, 93;
modernity, 96;
public esteem and character, 97-9;
relations with Charles, 99-100;
relations with Anne, 100;
and marriage, 104, 175;
carriage driving, 107;
and size of royal "firm", 119-20;
visits Germany, 128;
and Charles's marriage breakdown, 147;
in dreams, 177

Phillips, Captain Mark, 103

Phillips, Peter (son of Anne and Mark Phillips), 103

Ponsonby, Sir Henry, xxiv, 98

Porter, Henry, 56

Press Complaints Commission, 161

Private Eye (magazine), 61, 154

Reagan, Nancy, 59

Reenan, Cyril, 65
Reid, Sir James, 126
Republican Magazine, 144
republicanism, 1, 7, 150-4
Rhodes, Cecil, 169
Rhodes, Tom, 148-9
Richard I, King, 6
Richard II, King, 6
Richard III, King, 6
Roberts, Andrew, 133
Robinson, Mary, President of Ireland, xx, 49
Robsart, Amy, 57
Rothermere, Harold Sidney Harmsworth, 1st Viscount, 15
Rose, Kenneth: *George V*, 114
Royal Family: size and extent, 119-23;
name, 124
Royal Marriages Act (1772), 158
Royal Prerogative, 180-1
Ruskin, John, 110

Saddam Hussein, xix
Sampson, Anthony, 177
St John of Fawsley, Norman St John Stevas, Baron, xiii, 28, 36, 148
Sancha, Antonia de, 45
Scargill, Arthur, 113
Scargill, Mrs Arthur (Anne), 178
Select Committee on the Civil List, Report (1971), 28-37
Settlement, Act of (1701), 157
Seward, Ingrid, 77
Shea, Michael, 159
Sherrin, Ned, 164

Skinner, Dennis, 38, 144
Smith, John, 143
Sophia, Princess (Queen Victoria's aunt), 27
Spain, 2, 134
Spencer, Charles, 9th Earl (Diana's brother), 59
Spencer, Edward John, 8th Earl (Diana's father), 59n
Spencer, Lady Sarah (*later* McCorquodale; Diana's sister), 55, 59
Spectator (magazine), 56
Stamfordham, Arthur Bigge, Baron, 125
Stephen, King, 6
Stockmar, Baron Christian, 100
Stone, Norman, 164
Strachey, Lytton: *Queen Victoria*, xi
Sun, 29n, 45, 62-3, 71, 93, 116, 141, 144, 160, 163, 164
Sunday Telegraph, 165
Sunday Times, xxvi, 23, 54-8

Taj Mahal (India), 93
Taylor, Tim, 44
Tebbit, Norman (*later* Baron), 157
Teresa, Mother, 92
Thatcher, Margaret (*later* Baroness), 32, 38, 155
Thorpe, Jeremy, 31-2
Times, The, 78-9
"touching" (royal), 3
Townsend, Group Captain Peter, 7, 158

Townsend, Sue, 1
Tryon, Charles George Vivian Tryon, 2nd Baron, 31, 33
Turton, Sir Robin, 32

Vickers, Hugo, 22, 41, 122
Victoria, Queen: Strachey on, xi;
author's researches into, xii;
role, xii-xiv;
relations with children, xiv;
and children's marriages, xv-xvi;
and royal behaviour, xvii;
rumours over, xxii-xxiii, 110;
courtiers, xxiv;
greatness, 2;
and family, 3, 76;
on Edward VII's imprudence, 10
pays income tax, 25, 26, 143;
and moral example, 75, 76;
relations with daughters-in-law, 77n;
and press, 78;
political hostility to, 108;
accessibility, 121;
and racism, 126;
and ladies-in-waiting, 129;
personal economies, 135;
publishes *Journal*, 137;
resists change, 141;
marriage, 157;
succession, 166
Victoria, Princess (*later* Empress of Germany; Queen Victoria's eldest daughter), xiv, 123, 157

Villiers, Arthur, xviii
Villiers, Barbara, Duchess of Cleveland, 6

Wall, Mrs Michael, 126
Warwick, Frances, Countess of ("Daisy"), 11
Watts, Janet, 64
Wellington, Arthur Wellesley, 1st Duke of, xxiii
Wheeler, E. R., 35
Whitaker, James, 48, 56
Wigram, Clive, 1st Baron, 15
Wilhelm II, Kaiser, xii, 125
William II (Rufus), King, 6
William III, King, 6
William IV, King, 6, 30, 85, 135, 166
William, Prince (son of Charles and Diana), 45, 102, 147, 166, 170
Wilson, A. N., 19, 171
Wilson, Edgar, 144
Wilson, Harold (*later* Baron), 28, 33
Windsor, Edward, Duke of *see* Edward VIII, King
Windsor, Lord Frederick, 77
Windsor, Lady Gabriella, 77
Windsor, Lady Helen, 44
Windsor, Wallis, Duchess of (*formerly* Simpson), 13-16
Windsor Castle: 1992 fire, 30, 117, 119, 137-8, 142, 171;
restoration, 146
Wood, Russell, 32-3
Wood, W. A., 35

Woods, Rt Rev. Robert Wilmer, 91

Worsthorne, Sir Peregrine, 153

York, Prince Andrew, Duke of:
marriage breakdown, 5, 174;
view of Monarchy, 82;
Falklands service, 107;
at Windsor Castle fire, 117, 138;
in royal "firm", 120;
Queen pays expenses, 143;
as prospective regent, 166, 168

York, Sarah, Duchess of

("Fergie"): marriage break-down, 19, 45, 52-3, 71;
pays overdue builders' bill, 29n;
divorce pact with Diana, 54;
press photographs of, 62-3, 80;
taped telephone conversation, 65;
unpopularity, 66, 101;
hounded by press, 71;
Holden misjudges, 104;
crisicises Queen, 174

Ziegler, Philip, 105

LARGE PRINT

ISIS publish a wide range of books in large print, from fiction to biography. A full list of titles is available free of charge from the address below. Alternatively, contact your local library for details of their collection of ISIS books.

Details of ISIS unabridged audio books are also available.

Any suggestions for books you would like to see in large print or audio are always welcome.

ISIS
55 St Thomas' Street
Oxford OX1 1JG
(0865) 250333